GOOD NEW:
SATAN

A Gospel Look at Spiritual Warfare

Bob Bevington
Cruciform Press | January 2015

Dedicated to my beloved son Dave:

Your battle with demons
launched the quest to write this book,
and led to a deeper understanding of the gospel.

© 2015 by Bob Bevington. All rights reserved.
CruciformPress.com | info@CruciformPress.com

"The literature on spiritual warfare is often speculative and sensational. It's hard to know which authors to trust. But spiritual warfare is certainly an important biblical topic; from one perspective it is the central topic of the whole Bible. So it's important that believers get sober and reliable guidance on the subject. Bob Bevington's book is one of the most helpful. He has not put to rest all of the controversies in this area, but his book is reliable, biblical, and practical. It is easy to understand and challenges our spiritual complacency."

Dr. John M. Frame, Professor of Systematic Theology and Philosophy, Reformed Theological Seminary

"This is the best book I have ever read on this subject. It kept me up nearly an entire evening as I read it from cover to cover. I simply could not put it down. It is both highly Christ-centered and very practical, having the wonderful effect of focusing the reader's attention directly on Jesus while at the same time providing much useful help in the believer's battle against the enemy."

Mike Cleveland, Founder & President, Setting Captives Free

"*Good News About Satan* is filled with biblical reconnaissance and helpful insights for the conduct of spiritual warfare inherent in the life of every believer. In this concise treatment, Bob Bevington provides a stimulating analysis of the biblical data, drawing boundaries between the factual and fanciful, and grounding the reader firmly on the gospel of Jesus Christ."

Stanley D. Gale, author, *Warfare Witness: Contending with Spiritual Opposition in Everyday Evangelism* and *What is Spiritual Warfare?*

"Christians tend to fall into one of two camps when it comes to Satan and spiritual warfare: it becomes everything (resembling a Hollywood horror movie) or nothing (resembling a naturalistic worldview). Enter Bob Bevington, a wise teacher who decided to investigate for himself what the Bible really says—and doesn't say. The result is a careful and lively introduction to these important issues. The title is not a typo: understood in the grand storyline of Scripture, there really is good news about Satan. Read this book, prepare for battle, and rejoice in the victory that has been won and the glory that will shine more brightly."

    Justin Taylor, "Between Two Worlds" blogger at The Gospel Coalition; co-author, *The Final Days of Jesus*

"Spiritual warfare is an uncomfortable topic. Bob Bevington gives us the biblical 411 on our common enemy, the devil, without giving him the lead role of his book. The good news of Jesus Christ is the prominent message while Bevington distinguishes our relationship with the world, the flesh, and the devil. Parts of *Good News About Satan* have challenged me to dig deeper into what Scripture has to say in areas where I have questions. But most of all it magnifies Christ, equipping us with his Word and the application of it while further motivating me to share the gospel."

    Aimee Byrd, blogger; author, *Housewife Theologian*

"I am wary of books about Satan and spiritual warfare for numerous reasons. There seems to be too little of Christ the King when speaking about Satan the deceiver. But Bob Bevington is right, there is good news about the most maliciously evil being in the universe. The good news about Satan, says Bob, "begins with the recognition that Jesus Christ defeated the entire kingdom of darkness by his life, death, resurrection, and reign." Bob engages his readers with a simple exposition of what the Bible teaches about Satan and the believer's battle with this cruel and ruthless enemy. The best thing about Bob's book is that the counsel is saturated with the Word, and Christ is constantly presented as our victorious Champion. I found it simple, straightforward, and very helpful."

    Brian Borgman, author, *After They Are Yours, The Grace and Grit of Adoption*; co-author, *Spiritual Warfare, A Biblical and Balanced Approach*; pastor, Grace Community Church, Minden, NV

"Bob Bevington approaches a difficult subject with the precision of a surgeon. Using only the Bible as a source he is able to teach powerful truths concerning one of the most important areas of the Christian life: our relationship with the enemy. It's an area easily filled with misinformation and error in spite of it's critical nature. *Good News About Satan* is the first book I've read that applies the gospel to spiritual warfare so thoroughly. This is a tool I have long needed in my library. Like all great tools it is one I will use most on myself and then lend liberally to others."

Joe Coffey, author, *Smooth Stones: Bringing Down the Giant Questions of Apologetics*; co-author, *Red Like Blood: Confrontations with Grace*; Lead Pastor, Christ Community Chapel, Hudson, OH

Satan is real. Satan is dangerous. Satan is defeated. Those three notes form the chord that sounds through this clear, winsome, biblical book. In contrast to the many volumes that venture into unhelpful speculation about the nature of demons and extra-biblical methodology for engaging in spiritual warfare, here is a book that tenaciously sticks to God's revealed word with a steadfast focus on the triumphs of our God and King in the cross and resurrection of Christ. Read it, dress for battle, and stand in the victory that is yours in Christ!

Brian Hedges, author, *Active Spirituality: Grace and Effort in the Christian Life*, *Hit List: Taking Aim at the Seven Deadly Sins,* and other titles; Lead Pastor, Fulkerson Baptist Church, Niles, MI

"It is a rare book that both gives us our marching orders against the enemy and glorifies God in the mission. The good news about Satan is that God is always supreme. As the father of a son with severe autism, I need scripture to guide me through the dark valleys of disability. As a police officer who walks the front lines of the enemy's territory on a daily basis, I need to stay focused on my Savior and King. This book has made me better equipped to recognize the tactics of the accuser and face his fiery darts with solid, biblical, Christ-exalting confidence."

Greg Lucas, author, *Wrestling With An Angel*

CruciformPress

<u>**Our Books:**</u> Short and to the point—about 100 pages.
Clear. Concise. Helpful. Inspiring. Easy to read.
Solid authors. Gospel-focused. Local-church oriented.

<u>**Website Discounts:**</u>
  Print Books (list price $9.99)
    1-5 Books .... $8.45 each
    6-50 Books .... $7.45 each
    More than 50 Books .... $6.45 each
  Ebooks (list price $7.50)
    Single Ebooks .... $5.45 each
    Bundles of 7 Ebooks $35.00
    Ebook Distribution Program .... 6 pricing levels

<u>**Subscription Options:**</u> If you choose, print books or
ebooks delivered to you on a schedule, at a discount.
    Print Book Subscription *(list $9.99)* ...... $6.49 each
    Ebook Subscription *(list $7.50)* .... $3.99 each

Good News About Satan: A Gospel Look at Spiritual Warfare

Print / PDF **ISBN:** 978-1-936760-67-1
ePub **ISBN:** 978-1-936760-00-1
Mobipocket **ISBN:** 978-1-936760-68-8

Table of Contents

Psalm 121
My Help Comes from the LORD

A Song of Ascents

I lift up my eyes to the hills.
　　From where does my help come?
My help comes from the LORD,
　　who made heaven and earth.

He will not let your foot be moved;
　　he who keeps you will not slumber.
Behold, he who keeps Israel
　　will neither slumber nor sleep.

The LORD is your keeper;
　　the LORD is your shade on your right hand.
The sun shall not strike you by day,
　　nor the moon by night.

The LORD will keep you from all evil;
　　he will keep your life.
The LORD will keep
　　　your going out and your coming in
　　　from this time forth and forevermore.

FOREWORD

Good News About Satan is an important, much-needed book about spiritual warfare for several reasons:

First, it is a wake-up call to believers that all of us are involved in spiritual warfare whether we know it or not. I think my local church is above-average in its worship and Bible teaching, yet as I look around the congregation of about eight hundred people, I suspect that not more than one hundred would be consciously aware of the fact that we are all in a spiritual battle every day of our lives. The classic passage of Scripture on spiritual warfare, Ephesians 6:10–20, is not addressed to a small minority of super-Christians, but to every member of the body of Christ.

Second, it is a reminder that spiritual warfare involves more than our conflict with the devil and his angels. It is also a battle with the world and its myriads of temptations, and with our internal sinful flesh that is constantly looking for temptations to succumb to.

Third, it clearly identifies the weapons that Satan uses against us—deception, temptation, and accusation. It enables us to recognize these weapons so we can successfully resist them by faith in the power of Christ and by submission to his Word. It also exposes the pitfalls of the occult and false religions and instructs us about how to avoid them.

Fourth, and most important of all, it reminds us of the all-encompassing victory of Christ over and above every aspect of the kingdom of darkness, be it Satan, demons, the world, or our own sinful flesh. The glory of Christ is exalted as all-surpassing in this book, and Satan is put in his rightful place—defeated by the life, death, resurrection, and reign of the Son of God.

There is much more that I could say about the value of this book. It combines sound doctrinal exposition with helpful, practical suggestions to equip us to engage successfully in the many types of spiritual battles we encounter.

I pray that this book will be widely read and applied throughout our Christian community.

Jerry Bridges
Colorado Springs, Colorado
Author, *The Pursuit of Holiness*

INTRODUCTION
WAKE UP TO YOUR ENEMY

I sat in silence, staring at an open Bible. The wake-up call from God's Word could not have been more clear—we have an enemy who wants to tear us to pieces and consume us like fresh meat: "Be sober-minded; be watchful. Your adversary the devil prowls around like a roaring lion, seeking someone to devour" (1 Peter 5:8).

I had a personal reason for focusing on this passage. My son Dave had recently experienced a sustained and physically tangible demonic attack. A group of local Christians with experience in this area had helped him tremendously, and in a short time his life had changed dramatically. The outcome was amazing, but in the back of my mind I questioned whether all their methods were taken directly from the Bible. They graciously shared their source materials with me and I set out to thoroughly review them—a process that took several months, with my research eventually ranging far beyond their initial book list.

After evaluating dozens of books on the subject, I came to the conclusion that credible and decipherable books on spiritual warfare are extremely rare. Yet the need for such materials is great, even urgent. So I decided to seek God's enabling power to write an easy-to-read book on the subject—a book that would quote only one source: God's Word, the Bible, and never go beyond what is written.[1]

I'm glad I did because in the process I discovered an abundance of good news about Satan! I trust you will discover it, too, as you read these chapters.

Conflict from Cover to Cover

Spiritual warfare is one of the Bible's great themes, timeless in its relevance and essential in its significance. Its narrative on Satan and demons extends from cover to cover—beginning in Genesis 3 and ending in Revelation 20. In between, hundreds of verses offer astonishing insights. I will refer to most of them in this book.

The Bible warns against being ignorant of Satan's designs,[2] because the simplest way to be outwitted by him is to allow him to deceive you into believing either that he does not exist, that he has no designs, or that they don't matter. He does, and they do. Jesus definitely believed this. He believed in the personal existence of Satan and demons, and so should we. The proverbial ostrich with its head in the sand is completely defenseless against predators.

The Bible calls the devil *your adversary*. An adversary is a foe, an antagonist, a combatant, an *enemy*. It's important to note that when it comes to resisting this enemy, the Bible often uses the language of armed conflict, but without ever differentiating between genders. First Peter 5:8 was written to believers—male and female, young and old. If you are a Christian this means the devil is *your* enemy, and the "someone" the roaring lion seeks to devour is you. In the pages that follow I will repeatedly use the words *you* and *your* to help you keep this reality in mind. Please consider 1 Peter 5:8 to be your wake-up call in this area, and take it personally: Satan certainly does.

For centuries, students of the art of war have understood the first-best strategy to be: *know thy enemy*. It's common sense—before you enter a battle you must be prepared to recognize who and what you are up against. In our case, this is not an easy task. Your enemy is composed of bodiless spirits, physically invisible and masters of spiritual camouflage, "for even Satan disguises himself as an angel of light."[3] As difficult as it may be at times to identify Satan and demons, let there be no doubt they are a formidable enemy: "For we do not wrestle against flesh and blood, but against the rulers, against the authorities, against the cosmic powers over this present darkness, against the spiritual forces of evil in the heavenly places" (Ephesians 6:12). They have extraordinary supernatural powers that can easily exceed your own.

The Good News

But there is good news about Satan. It begins with the recognition that Jesus Christ defeated the entire kingdom of darkness by his life, death, resurrection, and reign. In fact, it was primarily his death that set us free. This can be clearly seen in Hebrews 2:14–15. "Since therefore the children share in flesh and blood, he himself likewise partook of the same things, that through *death* he might *destroy* the one who has the power of death, that is, the *devil*, and *deliver* all those who through fear of death were subject to lifelong slavery."

Yes, there is a cosmic clash. Yes, we are in the middle of it. Yes, we need to become equipped to recognize and resist the enemy. But through his death, Christ has destroyed the devil and delivered all believers from the enemy's grasp. If you are united to Jesus by genuine faith, his victory is your victory, too.

Ultimately, the good news about Satan is found in the all-surpassing glory of Jesus Christ:

> He humbled himself by becoming obedient to the point of death, even death on a cross. Therefore God has highly exalted him and bestowed on him the name that is above every name, so that at the name of Jesus every knee should bow, in heaven and on earth and under the earth, and every tongue confess that Jesus Christ is Lord, to the glory of God the Father. (Philippians 2:8–11)

For those who are in Christ, the radiance of his glory shines brightest against the blackest backdrop of the kingdom of darkness. This is how the bad news about Satan becomes the good news about Satan—his existence magnifies the glory of Christ, making us love, cherish, and revere Jesus all the more, both now and forever.

Bob Bevington
Hudson, Ohio

One
RECOGNIZE THEIR KINGDOM

God has a kingdom and Jesus is its King. In fact, he is the King of kings and the Lord of lords.[4] The *kingdom of God* is a major theme of the New Testament, one Jesus referred to more than a hundred times.[5]

But the Bible also speaks of another kingdom, a domain of darkness.[6] The clash between the kingdom of God and this renegade kingdom is known as *spiritual warfare*. As members of the kingdom of God, all Christians are unavoidably involved in the conflict—each one of us is commanded to engage in active resistance.[7]

Resistance requires knowing your enemy. And knowing your enemy begins with recognizing your enemy's leader.

Satan: The Fallen Day Star

Satan is the founder of the kingdom of darkness. Not an impersonal, evil force; not a metaphor for everything that is immoral, malicious, malignant, or malevolent—Satan is not a "what," but a "who." Not an "it," but a "he."[8] In fact, Satan is a supernatural, conscious, supremely evil spirit-being who is neither omniscient nor omnipresent. He has an individual identity and all the other characteristics of personhood including mind, will, and emotions. Ironically, he even has a "heart."[9]

One day Jesus sent seventy-two disciples on a mission trip. They returned with joy and astonishment reporting, "Lord, even the demons are subject to us in your name!" His response revealed something important about the leader of the demon forces: "I saw Satan fall like lightning from heaven"(Luke 10:17–18). Most of the seventy-two would have immediately understood the connection between Christ's statement about Satan and this fascinating Old Testament text:

> How you are fallen from heaven, O Day Star, son of Dawn!
> How you are cut down to the ground, you who laid the nations low!
> You said in your heart,
>> "I will ascend to heaven; above the stars of God
>> I will set my throne on high;
> I will sit on the mount of assembly in the far reaches of the north;
>> I will ascend above the heights of the clouds;
>> I will make myself like the Most High."
> (Isaiah 14:12–14)[10]

The King James Version of the Bible translates "Day Star" as *Lucifer*, and Jesus called him *Satan*, meaning "adversary."[11] They are one and the same being. We see from Scripture that he began as a powerful angel in the kingdom of heaven. At a point in time prior to Adam's sin,

Satan became dissatisfied with his position. Self-centered and puffed up with conceit, he intended to rise far above the other angels. His self-appointed mission? To place himself on equal terms with the Most High God. This was the epitome of rebellion, the ultimate expression of defiance against God's authority and glory.

With lightning speed, God cast Satan out of heaven. And yet Jesus later called him "the ruler of this world," Paul referred to him as "the god of this world," and John added, "the whole world lies in the power of the evil one."[12] Apparently, Satan retained significant power and →why? authority on the earth, where he's been prowling around like a roaring lion ever since.

Another Old Testament passage offers this direct quote from the Lord, shedding even more light on the fall of Satan:

> You were the signet of perfection, full of wisdom and perfect in beauty.
> You were in Eden, the garden of God;
> every precious stone was your covering...
> and crafted in gold were your settings and your engravings.
> On the day that you were created they were prepared.
> You were an anointed guardian cherub.
> I placed you; you were on the holy mountain of God;
> in the midst of the stones of fire you walked.
> You were blameless in your ways from the day you were created,
> till unrighteousness was found in you.

> In the abundance of your trade
> you were filled with *violence* in your midst, and you
> *sinned;*
>   *so I cast you as a profane thing* from the mountain
> of God,
>   and I *destroyed* you, O guardian cherub,
> from the midst of the stones of fire.
>   Your heart was *proud* because of your beauty;
>   you corrupted your wisdom for the sake of your
> splendor. (Ezekiel 28:12b–17a)[13]

Among Satan's other transgressions, he became guilty of raw, undiluted, primal pride. God made him beautiful, but Satan wanted the glory for this beauty. The Bible makes clear that he has never changed. He is still filled with violence, and still seeks to make himself like the Most High.

Demons: His Fallen Angels

The Book of Revelation contains another profound account of the fall of Satan. This one reveals that other angels joined in Satan's rebellion:

> Now war arose in heaven, Michael and his angels fighting against the dragon. And the dragon *and his angels* fought back, but he was defeated, and there was no longer any place for them in heaven. And the great dragon was thrown down, that ancient serpent, who is called the devil and Satan, the deceiver of the whole world—he was thrown down to the earth, *and his angels* were thrown down with him. (Revelation 12:7–9)

This is a depiction of all-out cosmic spiritual warfare: Michael and his angels vs. Satan and his angels. Satan's fallen angels are known in the Bible as demons, evil spirits, or unclean spirits.[14] They, like Satan, are wicked supernatural beings, powerful yet limited, conscious and personal, each one having an individual identity and location. Though they are immaterial in and of themselves, they can at times "enter" people and animals, as we will discuss later.[15]

Satan and demons individually and collectively exert a force like an army. Yet their kingdom is not a nebulous, ethereal "dark side." Rather, it is a league of fallen angels.

The Bible reveals that a huge number of angels are in existence ("innumerable," "myriad").[16] How many of them fell with Satan? Revelation 12:4 seems to indicate that one-third of all heaven's angels were swept down.[17] If that is true, there must be a lot of demons. One-third of innumerable is a lot! Are humans outnumbered by demons? It certainly seems to be possible. So while you probably have never encountered Satan himself, chances are you unknowingly encounter demons every day.

The Old Testament often portrays demons as the spirit-beings behind the false gods and idols that were worshiped by pagans and, at times, by the nation Israel: "[Israel] stirred [God] to jealousy with strange gods; with abominations they provoked him to anger. They sacrificed to *demons* that were no gods, to gods they had never known, to new gods that had come recently, whom your fathers had never dreaded" (Deuteronomy 32:16–17).[18]

Jesus taught about demons and frequently cast them out of people. If you believe in Jesus and take his words to be true, you cannot deny that demons exist on the earth. That would be tantamount to calling Jesus a liar.

These fallen angels are not a chaotic band of mercenaries. Rather, the kingdom of darkness is highly organized, for where there are "rulers," "authorities," and "powers" there must be subjects, underlings, and jurisdictions.[19] Satan acts as commander-in-chief of this vast demon militia, presiding over various levels of rank and command. This is your collective enemy, intent on leveraging sin in order (to the greatest extent possible) to stamp out your faith, destroy your life, and commandeer any glory God would ever get from you.

Humanity: His Subjects by Default

Have you ever been a member of the kingdom of darkness? You may be surprised to learn that the Bible's answer is yes. According to Scripture, all human beings are born into Satan's domain. Writing to Christians, Paul made this point painfully clear:

> And you were dead in the trespasses and sins in which you once walked, following the course of this world, *following the prince of the power of the air*, the spirit that is now at work in the sons of disobedience— among whom *we all* once lived in the passions of our flesh, carrying out the desires of the body and the mind, and were by nature children of wrath, *like the rest of mankind.* (Ephesians 2:1–3)

How can this be true? To answer this question we need to go all the way back to the Garden of Eden where God "created man in his own image."[20] Satan, the fallen hater of God, hated our first parents, too. He made them his targets. Please read this passage carefully because, as you will see, it has everything to do with all of us:

> Now the serpent[21] was more crafty than any other beast of the field that the LORD God had made. He said to the woman, "Did God actually say, 'You shall not eat of any tree in the garden'?" And the woman said to the serpent, "We may eat of the fruit of the trees in the garden, but God said, 'You shall not eat of the fruit of the tree that is in the midst of the garden, neither shall you touch it, lest you die.'" But the serpent said to the woman, "You will not surely die. For God knows that when you eat of it your eyes will be opened, and you will be like God, knowing good and evil"....she took of its fruit and ate, and she also gave some to her husband who was with her, and he ate. (Genesis 3:1–6)

The first Satan-to-human lie was, "You will not surely die." It was followed by the first half-truth, which also contained the first temptation: disobey God and you will become like him. Adam and Eve were *already* like God, for they were made in the image of God. But that was not enough. They desired to be "as" God, meaning equal to God. Adam and Eve fell to this specific temptation because they desired the same thing Satan wanted: to deify themselves *as the Most High*.

Humanity's first parents yearned for something impossible to attain, for the creature can never equal the uncreated Creator. At the end of the day, instead of becoming more like God, they became more like Satan. They attempted to hide from God. They were cursed by him and then banished from the Garden. Having been ejected from God's kingdom, there was only one alternative left: Adam and Eve entered the kingdom of darkness.[22]

From that point forward, everyone descended from Adam has inherited his sin nature.[23] At the core of our being we share Adam's (and Satan's) overwhelming desire to be the center of the universe. Can you feel that desire in yourself? The Bible says we are born with a tendency to sin, and before long all of us actually commit sin personally: "Therefore, just as sin came into the world through one man, and death through sin, and so death spread to all men because *all* sinned" (Romans 5:12).

This means all human beings are physically born spiritually dead. No exceptions. No matter how righteous you may feel right now, the fact remains that you were born into a fallen race of cosmic rebels under the domain of darkness. This should turn your stomach. But it gets worse. Your own sin, not Adam's, became your *personal* connection with the kingdom of darkness. This should make you downright queasy. If not, it's because sin is still powerfully active within you.

Welcome to the human race.

Recognizing your enemy's kingdom requires some understanding of your own part in it. You were a citizen in that fallen kingdom by default, and you later enlisted by committing your own sinful acts. But if you have been "delivered... from the domain of darkness and transferred... to the kingdom of his beloved Son, in whom [you] have redemption, the forgiveness of sins" and great reason to give "thanks to the Father, who has qualified you to share in the inheritance of the saints in light" (Colossians 1:12–14).

Welcome to the good news!

Two
RECOGNIZE THEIR ALLIES

Not all sin and evil is directly attributable to Satan or demons. The Bible reveals a triumvirate of separate, powerful, malicious, unholy allies that are aligned to wage spiritual warfare against you. These three are the *world*, the *flesh*, and the *devil*.²⁴ Blaming demons for everything that goes wrong ignores the *world* and the *flesh*. That is, it overlooks the fact that we live in a fallen world full of sinners, so we don't always need demonic help to make a mess of things!

While we can't know exactly to what degree the efforts of these three are coordinated "behind the scenes," we do know they share a common mission: to get you to turn your back on the Most High God. In any given instance of temptation, therefore, any or all of these three forces *might* be working together to oppose you, but it's not always easy to tell. It is not necessary to discern exactly the relative contribution of each, nor is it advisable to try. It is, however, strategically important to discern which of these three is taking the lead at any given time. Thankfully, the Bible helps us identify the unique weapons and distinct tactics each of these three typically deploys.

In this chapter we will discuss key Scriptures that provide insight to help you detect and overcome the influences of the world and the flesh.

The World: Temptation from Without

On the night before he was crucified, Jesus prayed to his Father for us[25] and repeated the same expression four times in three sentences: "The world has hated them because they are *not of the world*, just as I am *not of the world*. I do not ask that you take them out of the world, but that you keep them from the evil one. They are *not of the world*, just as I am *not of the world*" (John 17:14–16).

Jesus is "not of the world" and neither are we.[26] But notice he specifically asked the Father to *not* take us out of the world. He clearly intends for us to be *in* the world, but not *of* the world. Writing to believers, James puts it like this: "Do you not know that friendship with *the world* is enmity with God? Therefore whoever wishes to be a friend of *the world* makes himself an enemy of God"(James 4:4).

It's simple. If the world is your friend, God is your enemy. You cannot be friends with both.

The world hated Jesus, and if you are "not of the world" it hates you, too.[27] But like Satan, this unholy ally does not always appear to be hostile. If it seems like the world is merely playing a friendly game of tug-of-war, look out. In reality it is part of an all-out battle to control your heart and mind. Its chief tactic? *Promising the fulfillment of your desires through something other than a love relationship with God.* Thus John wrote this to believers: "Do not love the world or the things in the world. If anyone loves the world, the love of the Father is not in him. For all that is in the world — the desires of the flesh and the desires of the eyes and pride of life — is not from the Father but is from the world" (1 John 2:15–17).

We begin to love the world when we succumb to the temptation to think there's a good chance that what the world offers can satisfy certain desires. And since the world and its offerings are external to us, those temptations have to come to us in the form of messages. In our day, these messages pour ceaselessly from a gigantic set of megaphones called the Internet, film, television, radio, and print. These media — and the culture and subcultures they help produce — bombard us with a constant stream of desire-messages. These messages can be rude and raucous, or peacefully subliminal. They can be liberal or conservative, religious or secular, "Christian" or atheist, moral or immoral, distracting or seductive. But unless you're careful, most of these messages will tend to push God out of your conscious awareness and turn your attention and affection toward "the desires of the flesh, the desires of the eyes, and pride of life" — that is, toward anyone or anything *except* God.

How can you tell if a message is of the world? Here are three quick tests:

- When a message ignites your desire for instant gratification, think *the world.*
- When a message leads you to embrace a politically correct but unbiblical position such as pluralism[28] or relativism,[29] think *the world.*

- When a message compels you to pursue a folly-du-jour that has become popular with your peer group, think *the world*.

We cannot avoid exposure to the world's messages. So how should we respond to them? The Bible tells us, "Do not be conformed to this world, but be transformed by the renewal of your mind"(Romans 12:2–3a). But how?

Overcome the World with Better, Truer Messages

To begin with, there is a prerequisite to having a renewed mind, by virtue of which we can avoid being conformed to this world. Here it is in these three amazing sentences: "For everyone who has been born of God overcomes *the world*. And this is the victory that has overcome *the world*—our faith. Who is it that overcomes *the world* except the one who believes that Jesus is the Son of God?" (1 John 5:4–5). The prerequisite we see here is simple: you cannot overcome the corrupting influence of the world unless you first have saving faith in Jesus Christ.

In other words, authentic faith in the authentic Savior sets you up to overcome the universal human tendency to be squeezed into the world's mold. What great news!

So what do we do, as Christians, to take advantage of this God-given ability to renew our minds and thus resist the world? We must apply the Bible's command, "Do not be overcome by evil, but overcome evil with good" (Romans 12:21). Practically speaking, this means limit your exposure to the world's ungodly messages and bombard your own heart and mind with ultimate truth by regularly dwelling on:

- God's message, the gospel[30]
- God's Son, Jesus Christ[31]
- Whatever is true, honorable, just, pure, lovely, and commendable[32]

Eventually, as the process of renewing your mind continues, you can achieve considerable freedom from the world and its ungodly influence. Paul wrote, "But far be it from me to boast except in the cross of our Lord Jesus Christ, by which *the world* has been crucified to me, and I to *the world*" (Galatians 6:14).

Becoming crucified to the world is a painful process that will continue as long as we remain in these bodies.[33] At the same time, we can and should be making real progress on a regular basis toward being freed from the world's corrupting influences.

Jesus himself understood that being "in the world, but not of the world" would produce a transformed life, but not an easy life. Here is his message to you: "I have said these things to you, that in me you may have peace. In *the world* you will have tribulation. But take heart; I have overcome *the world*" (John 16:33).[34]

The Flesh: Temptation from Within

The Bible warns us of a third adversary that is both allied with and closely related to the world and the devil. But where the world is external to us, this evil ally is much closer than you can imagine. It's called *the flesh*, and it wages war against your soul.[35]

In this context, *the flesh* is not your physical human body.[36] It's your fallen nature, the part of your inner being that continues to be infected with a pathological inclination toward sinful selfishness, sensuality, and pride. Paul experienced this and explained: "For while we were living *in the flesh*, our sinful passions, aroused by the law, were at work in our members to bear fruit for death. I am *of the flesh*, sold under sin.…For I do not do what I want, but I do the very thing I hate" (Romans 7:5, 14b–15).

Paul does what he hates because, although he is a Christian, he is nevertheless "*of* the flesh," and the flesh induces him to sin. Can you feel the pull of the flesh as it battles against your soul, causing you to sin, even sometimes when you don't really want to? It's a deadly war because the wages of sin is death.[37]

How can you tell when your flesh is on the attack?

- When you're wrestling with sinful cravings, whether it's an ungodly appetite for food, recognition, security, or pleasure, think *the flesh*.
- When desires are inflamed and you're fighting the urge to fulfill them in ways that disregard and dishonor God, think *the flesh*.
- When you're gripped by an impulse to satisfy your self-centered, self-indulgent, self-reliant, prideful inclinations, think *the flesh*.

How influential is the flesh? Influential enough to single-handedly pollute and even defile a person. As Jesus put it, "For *from within*, out of the heart of man, come evil thoughts, sexual immorality, theft, murder, adultery, coveting, wickedness, deceit, sensuality, envy, slander, pride, foolishness. All these evil things come *from within*, and they defile a person" (Mark 7:21–23).

Satan and the world attack us from the outside with messages that appeal to our flesh. The flesh is their "mole" on the inside—their strategic ally that attacks us from within, sometimes even without the provocation of messages. In fact, if God were to put an impenetrable hedge around you to keep the devil and the world completely away, you would still continue to sin in thought, word, deed, and motive.[38] (If you doubt this, please consider the definitions of murder and adultery Jesus gave in the Sermon on the Mount.[39]) The flesh is an enemy cloaked in the ultimate disguise: it is woven into the fabric of your being.

How powerful is the flesh? Powerful enough to oppose your will and win! Even the great apostle Paul recognized that in and of himself he was unable to resist it: "For I know that nothing good dwells in me, that is, in my flesh. For I have the desire to do what is right, but *not the ability* to carry it out" (Romans 7:18). If this is true of Paul, it is true of you, too. All-out, white-knuckled, human exertion is like a BB gun against the nuclear warheads your flesh deploys against you on any given day.

So if your best efforts are not enough, how can you avoid defeat?

Overcome the Flesh in the Power of the Son and the Spirit

It's worth saying again: you can give up trying to resist the flesh in your own strength. Telling yourself to *just say no* is doomed to fail eventually, and probably pretty quickly.[40] Paul wrote, "For though we walk in the flesh, we are not waging war according to the flesh"(2 Corinthians 10:3). In other words, when it comes to battling the flesh, you cannot fight fire with fire. Thanks be to God, he provided a better way: a divine Person, an omnipotent ally, the ultimate Helper. God provided the Holy Spirit. He, too, is much closer than you can imagine, for he indwells every authentic Christian.[41] The tide is turned in your battle against the flesh when you draw on the Spirit's enabling power. As Paul wrote, "Walk by *the Spirit*, and you will not gratify the desires of the flesh" (Galatians 5:16).

The presence of the Holy Spirit in us means we do not *have to* sin: "For the law of the Spirit of life has set you free in Christ Jesus from the law of sin and death…. So then, brothers, we are debtors, not to the flesh, to live according to the flesh. For if you live according to the flesh you will die, but if by the Spirit you put to death the deeds of the body, you will live" (Romans 8:2, 12–13).

This is all very encouraging. But here's the rub. Your flesh not only wages war against your soul, it also opposes the Spirit of God: "For the desires of *the flesh* are against *the Spirit*, and the desires of *the Spirit* are against *the flesh*, for these are opposed to each other, to keep you from doing the things you want to do" (Galatians 5:17).

The Spirit is working in us, but sin remains active in us, too. If we always walked by the Spirit, the flesh would lose every battle. But there is constant inner conflict and the desires of the flesh have their way with us far too often. Like Paul, we cry out, "Wretched man that I am! Who will deliver me from this body of death?"

Thanks be to God, for he provided the ultimate Deliverer, another divine Person and omnipotent ally, the Savior, Jesus Christ.[42] By drawing on the saving power of Christ we are delivered—not from an *inclination* to sin, but from the *condemnation* we deserve for our flesh-inspired sin: "For God has done what the law, weakened by *the flesh*, could not do. By sending his own Son in the likeness of sinful *flesh* and for sin, he condemned sin in the *flesh*" (Romans 8:3).

Ironically, Christ became our deliverer by taking on flesh, except he did it sinlessly.[43] When he bore our sin in his body on the cross, he completely and permanently delivered us from the condemnation and death penalty we deserve.[44] And one fine day he will also completely and permanently deliver us from the *presence* of our sin.

Meanwhile, as we are slowly being transformed[45] by our two great allies, the Son and the Spirit, we can get to the point where at times we resonate with Paul when he wrote, "I have been crucified with Christ. It is no longer I who live, but Christ who lives in me. And the life I now live in *the flesh* I live by faith in the Son of God, who loved me and gave himself for me"(Galatians 2:20).

God the Father did not expect us to have a daily showdown with our flesh, apply the law, and just say *No* to its passions.[46] He provided the Deliverer (God the Son) and the Helper (God the Spirit), whose combined power makes the biggest nuclear mushroom cloud that the flesh can generate seem like a powder puff by comparison.

Three
RECOGNIZE THEIR WEAPONS

The Bible calls them *flaming darts*. That may not sound especially threatening, but if your shield of faith fails, one flaming dart can set your whole life ablaze.[47] Those darts have reduced marriages to ashes, burned down relationships, torched entire ministries, and even fanned the flames of despair that have led many to commit suicide. These weapons are not to be taken lightly.

The enemy has three major kinds of darts to deploy against our souls: *deception*, *temptation*, and *accusation*. All three are used with stealth and cunning, like the work of a committed arsonist who is able to ignite an entire home by starting with a bit of dry tinder and a single match. The fire grows from within, but before long the entire structure is engulfed in flames.

Where there's smoke, there's fire. The purpose of this chapter is to expose the enemy's fiery darts and help you learn to extinguish them before they consume your thoughts, your desires, your identity, and potentially your faith.

Deception Targets Your Mind

Jesus made the following points about the devil. "He…
does not stand in the truth, because there is no truth in
him. When he lies, he speaks out of his own character, for
he is a liar and the father of lies" (John 8:44).

Wherever you find spiritual deception, the enemy
is near at hand. Satan and demons are more interested in
putting lies in your heart than fang marks in your flesh.
Here is an astonishing statement, supported by Scripture,
and one you would be wise to take note of: the father of
lies has demonstrated the ability to implant lies into the
hearts of men and women.

Consider the case of Ananias. The Bible states plainly
that Satan *filled [his] heart* to tell a lie.[48] And in the case
of Judas, we read, "During supper, when the devil had
already *put it into the heart* of Judas Iscariot, Simon's son,
to betray him" (John 13:2).

You can think of a person's "heart" as the center of
his or her mind, will, and emotions. How does the enemy
"put" ideas into a heart? How does he "fill" a heart to
become a deceiver like himself? The Bible provides some
insight here: "But I am afraid that as the *serpent deceived*
Eve by his cunning, *your thoughts will be led astray* from a
sincere and pure devotion to Christ" (2 Corinthians 11:3).

Look carefully. There are circumstances under
which the serpent, namely Satan, can "lead" (guide, steer,
prompt, provoke) your thoughts. And remarkably, this is
not merely true of unbelievers. It can happen to believers,
too. The verse above was written to Christians!

Can the enemy cause you to "see" images or "hear"
words in your head? The Bible does not specifically
answer that question.[49] And yet it does make one thing

perfectly clear. In a passage written in the context of spiritual warfare, the Bible commands you to take *every thought* captive to obey Christ.[50] Does this refer to the real thoughts you experience in your real head? Of course it does. Renegade ideas inspired by the enemy need to be captured and neutralized.

If you assume *your* thoughts are not susceptible to the impact of the enemy's deceptions, consider this statement the Bible makes about King David, a man after God's own heart:[51] "Then Satan stood against Israel and *incited* David to number Israel" (1 Chronicles 21:1).[52] Exactly how can Satan stir up a person like David to think about something sinful and then go out and do it? We are not told, and yet the following points appear to be reliable:

- The enemy seldom uses audible nonhuman voices to try to deceive us.
- The external and internal messages conveyed by Satan's allies — the world and the flesh — can provoke thoughts and emotions that lead us to embrace lies.
- Circumstances can be supernaturally orchestrated by the enemy in such a way as to deceive us by the power of suggestion.

Speculation aside, the Bible provides amazing insights into the process by which satanic lies can take thoughts captive:

> For although they knew God, they did not honor him as God or give thanks to him, but they became *futile in their thinking*, and their *foolish hearts were darkened* ... they *exchanged the truth about God*

35

for a lie and worshiped and served the creature rather than the Creator, who is blessed forever! Amen. (Romans 1:21–22, 25)

The most basic truth about the Creator is this: he is God and we are not. When we fail to regard and honor him, our thoughts become futile, thwarted, foolish, and broken. Meanwhile our hearts become dark and open to satanic deceptions that can lead to a disconnect from reality, a cosmic insanity in which we literally worship and serve mere creatures instead of the real God who made us.

As you will see in the next section, this is the fundamental lie underneath all temptations.

Temptation Targets Your Desires

The first chapter of James provides keen insight into the insidious way the fiery dart of temptation attacks. Interestingly, temptation always takes advantage of desires that already exist inside of you: "But each person is *tempted* when he is *lured and enticed by his own desire*. Then desire when it has conceived gives birth to sin, and sin when it is fully grown brings forth death"(James 1:14–15).

The human heart is like a kettle of stew on a hot stovetop, bubbling up desires of various kinds and intensities, and not all of them godly.[53] Your own desires do the actual luring and enticing. The tempter merely adds the stimulus, which is always some form of lie or half-truth. No wonder the very next statement from James is, "Do not be *deceived*, my beloved brothers," to which he immediately adds, "every good gift and every perfect gift is from above, coming down from the Father of lights

with whom there is no variation or shadow due to change"
(James 1:16–17).

God alone is the fountain of *all* good things. He
intends for *all* of your desires to be met in and through him
exclusively.[54] But let's be clear on what that sentence means.
Note that the context of James 1:14–15 is *temptation,
desires*, and *deception*. Whether it's your desire for comfort,
security, significance, pleasure, acceptance, or approval,
God is the only source of true and permanent fulfillment
of every one of your deep longings, including all of these.
And since you cannot see God, as you look to him to
satisfy your desires, you must approach him by *faith*.[55]

But then, along comes the enemy to deceive you into
believing that one of your heart's desires would be better
fulfilled by placing your faith (trust, reliance, dependency)
in something that isn't God. Once you've embraced
this deception, your desire will become a renegade one,
conceiving and giving birth to sin, "for whatever does not
proceed from *faith* is sin" (Romans 14:23).

So here's a vital principle:

*Your battle with temptation is ultimately a battle for your
faith — specifically, your faith in God as the all-surpassing
treasure of your life.*

Every temptation seeks to draw your attention to
some false treasure. So to extinguish a spiritual fiery dart
it is very nearly essential to first identify the specific desire
and deception involved. These questions can help, and
as a matter of both immediate and long-term strategy in
your battle against sin, it is best to commit the answers to
writing:

- Which of my desires is under attack by the enemy's weapon of temptation?
- What lie or half-truth am I being tempted to believe?
- What sinful substitute or false treasure am I being tempted to accept in an effort to meet this desire?
- Am I willing to embrace God's truth and trust him to meet this desire in his own time and his own way?

After you have prayerfully clarified the answers to these questions, share them with a pastor or close friend. Together, ask God to enable you to:

- Repent of your ungodly desire.
- Get on a Godward path of faith and obedience.
- Be empowered to take the deceptive thoughts captive the next time.

Consider the Lord's Prayer. Jesus taught us to ask that God lead us not into temptation, implying that he sometimes *does*.[56] But let's clarify what this means. God does not tempt us directly, since trying to persuade someone to sin is itself sinful. But God does "test" us.[57] This "testing" can involve granting the enemy permission to expose us to temptation. God does this not because he's trying to learn something about us—it's not so that *he* can learn and grow, but so that *we* can. God's testing of us is always for our good, because the battles with temptation that he hand-picks for us give us opportunity to grow in one or more of several different areas. Here are just some of them:

- We can be informed or reminded of a particular area of weakness.

- We can learn to cry out to God for help more consistently.
- We can learn to depend on his enabling power rather than our willpower.
- We can have our faith built up as we see victory over the temptation.

Simply put, Satan tempts us in order to destroy our faith; God tests us in order to build it.[58] Jesus concluded his lesson in prayer with, "but deliver us from evil." Deliverance means God does it all. We simply receive the blessing by faith. Jesus, the Deliverer, is ready, willing, and able to deliver us. What are we waiting for? Let's ask!

Consider Jesus.[59] He met the full-force onslaught of the enemy's fiery darts, and yet he did not succumb to a single temptation.[60] As you are well aware, the intensity of a temptation grows and grows until we finally give in to it, and then it goes away for a season. But unlike us, Jesus never gave in. This means the level of temptation Jesus endured had to be unimaginable to us. And since "he himself has suffered when tempted, he is able to help those who are being tempted" (Hebrews 2:18). This is extremely good news for believers battling with temptation.

Jesus told his disciples, "watch and pray that you may not enter into temptation. The spirit indeed is willing, but the flesh is weak" (Matthew 26:41). God's throne of grace always awaits the prayer of the weak, so draw near by faith in Jesus.

For we do not have a high priest who is unable to sympathize with our weaknesses, but one who in every respect has been tempted as we are, yet without

sin. Let us then with confidence draw near to the
throne of grace, that we may receive mercy and find
grace to help in time of need. (Hebrews 4:15-16).

Plus, the way of escape is always available if you
will pray the prayer of the tempted, so enter that way of
escape by faith in Jesus' precious promises.

No temptation has overtaken you that is not
common to man. God is faithful, and he will not let
you be tempted beyond your ability, but with the
temptation he will also provide the way of escape,
that you may be able to endure it. (1 Corinthians
10:13)

He has granted to us his precious and very great
promises, so that through them you may become
partakers of the divine nature, having escaped from
the corruption that is in the world because of sinful
desire. (2 Peter 1:4)

As you can see, prayer is our lifeline to good news
when we are on the brink of entering into temptation.

Accusation Targets Your Conscience

The Bible calls Satan "the accuser of the brothers" and
then makes an intriguing statement. It says "he [Satan]
accuses them day and night before our God."[61]

Are you an authentic believer? Then without even
knowing it, at this very moment, you could be named as
a defendant in the ultra-supreme courtroom, where God

the Father presides as the Judge.[62] Satan is there, too, as the prosecutor. He presents an ironclad case against you, enumerating every single one of your sins, and demanding you be condemned.[63] Is he telling the truth for once? After all, the evidence *is* conclusive; you are truly guilty as charged.

Or are you?

The resurrected Christ is also in the "courtroom" (metaphorically speaking). He appears on your behalf as your advocate, mediator, and intercessor.[64] In essence, he is your divine defense attorney. His rebuttal might sound something like this: "Your Honor, we admit the defendant committed these offenses. But as his representative, I have already paid the death penalty for those sins in my body on the tree. There is therefore now no condemnation left for him to bear. I move that the defendant be declared *not guilty*."[65]

The Judge is just. He will not extract payment for the same sin twice. If the punishment was meted out on your representative, he will not mete it out again on you as well. Furthermore, the record of your sins was expunged at the cross at the very moment Jesus uttered the words, "it is finished."[66] Therefore the accuser's evidence, while true, is thrown out as inadmissible. The final verdict is pronounced: *forever not guilty*, and the gavel comes down.

This is the gospel of Jesus Christ. It offers forgiveness, reconciliation, and peace to undeserving sinners. It is pure grace.[67] But if you fail to properly and fully apply it—which we all do on a regular basis—look out! The accuser will assault your conscience in an attempt to get you to condemn yourself, even if God does not.

We have already seen that temptation cannot exist without deception. The same is true when it comes to accusation against Christians. Accusation aims to deceive you into believing that the Savior's death did not pay the debt for *all* of your sin and remove *all* of your guilt—that you need to pay some of the price and bear some of the guilt on your own.

So here's another vital principle:

Your battle with accusation is ultimately a battle for your faith—specifically, your faith in Christ as the all-sufficient sacrifice for your sins.

Satan's accusations are so devious they can seem like they are coming from God. The Devil can act as a counterfeit Holy Spirit, who is himself the Person of the triune God who illuminates our hearts with respect to matters of sin, righteousness, and judgment.[68] Both the enemy and the Spirit can cause you to experience a guilty conscience.[69] Therefore, part of becoming trained for spiritual warfare involves learning to discern between satanic accusation and gospel-informed conviction by the Spirit. Here are some ways to recognize the difference:

- When your guilty conscience rivets your attention to yourself, it's the enemy. When it shifts your focus to the cross, it's the Spirit.
- When your guilty conscience moves you toward self-loathing, shame, discouragement, and despair, it's the enemy. When it moves you toward confession, repentance, reconciliation, and renewed fellowship with God, it's the Spirit.[70]
- When your guilty conscience results in a more isolated, phony, fearful, sinful life, it's the enemy.

When it results in an increasingly accessible, transparent, assured, holy life, it's the Spirit.

The Spirit of God alerts you to the damnable nature of your sin, and that can be daunting. But he is also your Comforter.[71] He reminds you that as a redeemed sinner you are an adopted and beloved child of God.[72]

Satan will continue to accuse you day and night before the throne of God. And when you forget the gospel, the fiery darts of accusation will continue to assail your conscience. But as you will see, this will not go on forever.

Therefore, always keep your Savior in sight, remembering *who* it was on the cross, *what* he accomplished there, and *why*.[73] Remember your identity in Christ: you are his, and in spite of the onslaught of accusation, no one can snatch you out of his hand.[74]

Four
RECOGNIZE THEIR LIMITATIONS

Let there be no doubt about it. Satan and demons are created beings, as this verse clearly states: "For by [God's beloved Son] all things were created, in heaven and on earth, visible and invisible, whether thrones or dominions or rulers or authorities—all things were created through him and for him" (Colossians 1:16).

Fallen angels, like all created beings, are in no way equal to the uncreated and unique I AM, who declares: "I am God, and there is no other."[75] Many people think of Satan as the counterpart of God, as if he is an equal but opposite evil force. As if God and Satan are two fire hoses facing each other with equivalent, offsetting thrust. But that is nowhere near the truth, for the combined forces of the entire kingdom of darkness are no match for the Father, Son, and Holy Spirit.

Satan and demons are creatures. All creatures have limitations, and theirs include the four monumental ones we will cover in this chapter.

Limited in Power

Satan is not omnipotent, God alone is. God is referred to as "the Almighty" fifty-eight times in Scripture. *Nowhere* in the Bible is Satan given that designation. God's power is always infinite; Satan's is always finite. In fact, it is not merely finite—the Bible reveals that the power of the fallen angels was greatly diminished by the debilitating effects of their sin: "And the angels who did not stay within their own position of authority, but left their proper dwelling, he *has kept in eternal chains* under gloomy darkness until the judgment of the great day" (Jude 6).

Thus it has been said that a demon, or even Satan himself, is "a creature on a leash." While this is true, we must not become cavalier about spiritual warfare. When we read this verse in context we discover an astonishing statement two sentences later: "But when the archangel Michael, contending with the devil, was disputing about the body of Moses, he did not presume to pronounce a blasphemous judgment, but said, 'The Lord rebuke you'" (Jude 9).

The archangel Michael is among the most powerful angels. And yet when engaged in spiritual warfare, he did not personally attempt to revile, denounce, or lambaste Satan. Instead, he appealed to the Lord to do the rebuking. As we will see in chapter eight, all believers who are dependent on God's enabling power definitely have a degree of authority to resist and contend with Satan and demons. Some are even endowed with special gifts of spiritual discernment. But we must all stay within our limits: God holds the leash, we do not.

When Jesus looked the devil in the eye and said, "Be

gone," Satan departed.[76] He can cast out demons, even by the thousands, with a single word.[77] That's the power of the Son of God. He did it with ease. And he did it to make a point, an announcement of massive importance, saying, "if it is by the finger of God that I cast out demons, then *the kingdom of God has come upon you*" (Luke 11:20). The Prince of Peace had arrived on the face of the planet and the prince of darkness was no match for him. Things would never be the same.

What about us? Can we cast out demons with the flick of a finger? No. But as citizens of the kingdom of God we can appeal to the Almighty One at any time and in any place where we encounter satanic forces. If the archangel did it, so should we.

The Creator has power over every type of creature including humans, angels, and demons. There are no exceptions. "Ah, Lord GOD! It is you who have made the heavens and the earth by your great power and by your outstretched arm! Nothing is too hard for you" (Jeremiah 32:17). This is very good news. When we are "strong in the Lord" and in the "strength of his might" and have "put on the whole armor of God,"[78] we can overcome the enemy. "For he who is in [us] is greater than he who is in the world" (1 John 4:4). And because the power comes from God alone, he alone gets all the glory when the enemy retreats.[79]

Limited in Knowledge

I have had days when it seemed like the enemy knew exactly what I was thinking. Maybe you have had those days too. You feel vulnerable to a specific sinful desire and then—boom—there it is right in your face. It could be anything from sexual temptation to chocolate cake. At times the presentations are too personalized to be reasonably chalked up to coincidence. They seem more like targeted spiritual attacks, making us wonder…*how much does the enemy know?*

Satan is not omniscient, God alone is. "The LORD knows the thoughts of man, that they are but a breath" (Psalm 94:11). He even knows the words that will come out of your mouth before you say them.[80] Not only can God read our minds, he alone knows *all* things:

> He determines the number of the stars;
> he gives to all of them their names.
> Great is our Lord, and abundant in power;
> *his understanding is beyond measure.* (Psalm 147:4–5)

> Have you not known? Have you not heard?
> The LORD is the everlasting God, the Creator of the ends of the earth.
> He does not faint or grow weary; *his understanding is unsearchable.* (Isaiah 40:28)

The Bible does not make statements like these about Satan or demons. They are fallen *angels*, and all angels have limited knowledge. Peter wrote that there are "things into which angels long to look,"[81] indicating they do not know all things.

God alone knows precisely what is to come. This is apparent in many places in the Bible, and is clearly seen here: "I am God, and *there is none like me*, declaring the end from the beginning, and from ancient times things not yet done" (Isaiah 46:9–10).

If Satan and demons have limited knowledge, why does it sometimes seem as if the enemy can read our minds? Here are some possible explanations:

- Scripture gives us no reason to believe that angels (holy or fallen) need sleep or sustenance, like we do, in order to remain active. Nor does it indicate they are born or die. Therefore we can assume that the same demons you encounter in spiritual warfare today have had thousands of years to study human nature and become experts on the subject—and the subject is you.
- The best inferences from Scripture suggest that Satan and demons can see and hear us, and can see and hear everything we can see and hear.[82]
- If this is true it means they can run surveillance on your actions and listen to your words. They can see the screen of your computer, mobile phone, and GPS. They can observe which keyboard buttons you push, and before long they pretty much know what pushes your buttons.

Are specific demons familiar with your behavior patterns, vulnerabilities, and weaknesses? Have you become predicable enough for them to customize their approach to tempting you? If so, they essentially do know what you are thinking. And even though they can't literally read your mind, they can literally lead your thoughts.

Speculation aside, we can be sure Satan and his minions are highly intelligent. While their knowledge is clearly limited, it is probably also quite extensive, with their insight into human nature one of their biggest advantages.

Limited in Time and Space

Have you ever had one of those days when there was static, conflict, frustration, and confusion all around? When it seemed like no matter which way you turned, you were hindered by an invisible but real hostility? A day when it seemed as if Satan was everywhere?

But Satan is not omnipresent, God alone is. The Bible repeatedly declares he is present everywhere all the time. Here is one example: "Can a man hide himself in secret places so that I cannot see him? declares the LORD. Do I not fill heaven and earth? declares the LORD" (Jeremiah 23:24).[83]

The Bible does not make statements like this about Satan. On the contrary, we read verses like the one below which indicates that Satan—like angels and humans—can only be in one place at a time: "The LORD said to Satan, 'From where have you come?' Satan answered the LORD and said, 'From going to and fro on the earth, and from walking up and down in it'" (Job 1:7).

An omnipresent being does not need to go "to and fro" and "up and down" on the earth since he's already everywhere. Rest assured, Satan is not omnipresent. So where is he?

"God did not spare angels when they sinned, but cast them into hell and committed them to chains of gloomy darkness to be kept until the judgment" (2 Peter 2:4). Satan and demons were exiled to a location called *hell*, and yet dozens of other Bible verses indicate they are also present on the earth.[84] This means they are apparently free to travel, chains and all, between hell and earth. *Chains* is a metaphor showing that their movements are ultimately controlled by the will of their divine jailer. This is yet another indication that the enemy is not omnipresent.

If Satan cannot be present everywhere in person, how is he able to clash with people all over the world at the same time? You probably know the answer. Like a five-star general, he dispatches his demons to strategic places where they carry out his orders. If at times it *seems* like Satan is omnipresent it's because there are large numbers of demons at his disposal. They are ready, willing, and able to be deployed. Most likely it is they, not him, whom you encounter in spiritual warfare. There is not a demon behind every bush, but could an evil spirit be in your presence as you read this sentence? Possibly. The reason? Satan does not want to be recognized, and this book exposes him.

If, as the Bible says, the enemy will flee from anyone who submits to God and resists the devil,[85] then we can find "places" that are completely free from the presence of the enemy. Jesus experienced them[86] and so can we. This, too, is part of the good news of the gospel.

Limited in Authority

Satan is not the sovereign of the world, God alone is. God has the power and the right to govern all things, and he does. He always "works all things according to the counsel of his will."[87] As mere creatures, Satan and demons can go about their wicked business only with God's permission and within God's appointed limits.

The Book of Job is a fascinating place to see this. The story opens with a conversation between God and Satan. They are discussing Job, a righteous and prosperous servant of God.[88]

> Satan: "Stretch out your hand and touch all that he has, and he will curse you to your face."

> The LORD: "Behold, all that he has is in your hand.
> Only against him do not stretch out your hand."
> Satan: "Stretch out your hand and touch his bone and
> his flesh, and he will curse you to your face."
> The LORD: "Behold, he is in your hand; only spare his
> life."

Satan recognized that he needed God's permission before he could raise his hand with evil intent against Job. God consented, but also limited the categories and the extent of the destructive forces Satan could use. The implications of this for us are huge. It means God is ultimately in control of all things, including Satan. But if this is true, why did Jesus declare Satan to be the ruler of this world?[89]

Satan has God-given but limited jurisdiction on the earth. We know this because Jesus also declared, "All authority in heaven and on earth has been given to me" (Matthew 28:18). Satan's authority is not ultimate, Christ's is. Therefore, when he "commands the unclean spirits, they obey *him*,"[90] not Satan.

Satan challenged these truths when he tempted Jesus in the wilderness. He "showed him all the kingdoms of the world in a moment of time, and said to him, 'To you I will give all this authority and their glory, for it has been delivered to me, and I give it to whom I will. If you, then, will worship me, it will all be yours'" (Luke 4:5–7).

Jesus refused. He knew Satan's claim was a lie, for the devil has never had the ability to transfer the authority and glory of all the world's kingdoms to whomever he wills. In fact, the Bible declares, "The Most High rules the kingdom of men and gives it to whom he will" (Daniel 4:17). And he wills to give it to Jesus.[91]

This is extremely good news for us. It means two things. When it seems like Satan is winning, he's not. And when it seems like your world is spinning out of control, it isn't. "Our God is in the heavens; he does *all* that *he* pleases" (Psalm 115:3). The best good news is coming up in chapter six, but before we get there, we must first consider one more element of spiritual warfare.

Five
RECOGNIZE THEIR MANEUVERS

The first brothers, Cain and Abel, knew the LORD and worshipped him by offering sacrifices. In fact, God spoke directly to Cain on more than one occasion, including the time he warned Cain about his anger. But Cain did not heed God's warning. Instead, he killed his brother.[92]

The Bible tells us, "We should not be like Cain, who was *of the evil one* and murdered his brother" (1 John 3:12). It is not surprising to learn that cold-blooded murderers like Cain are of the evil one. However, you might be surprised to learn that "Whoever makes a practice of sinning is *of the devil*" (1 John 3:8). Do you know people who appear to practice sin actively, without any real efforts to resist it? They may well be of the devil. Do *you* make a practice of sinning? If so, this is very, very bad news.

Please resist the temptation to skip ahead to the next chapter. Yes, there is extremely good news to be found there. But in order to fully appreciate it, you first need to recognize the enemy's maneuvers. His desire is to get you to sin, bind you to sin, destroy your faith, and ultimately control your mind and body.

Sin: From Toeholds to Strangleholds

The enemy's goal behind every deception, temptation, accusation, and allied attack is always the same—to inspire and prompt human sin. Satan knows, and so should you, that every single one of your known sins is a verifiable act of treason against the kingdom of God. You are solely responsible for it, and you will be held account-able for it.[93] Do not think for a second that you can get off the hook by blaming Satan for your sin.

Deliberate sin is satanic, "For rebellion is as the sin of divination" (1 Samuel 15:23). When humans intention-ally sin, they are clearly *not* bearing the image of a holy God. Instead, they take on the image of Satan, the original sinner. And when they make a practice of sinning, they bear his image to such an extent they are considered, tragi-cally, to be "of the devil."

Of course, all authentic believers sin in thought, word, deed, and motive. Does that mean genuine Christians are also of the devil? No. Only the one who *makes a practice of sinning* is of the devil.[94] So the question is: what does it mean to *practice* sin?

Jesus provided much clarity on this question when he said, "Truly, truly, I say to you, everyone who *practices sin is a slave to sin*" (John 8:34). A slave is someone who is under the dominion or control of another. To practice sin, then, means to live in a state of being surrendered to sin, over-whelmed by its power, and unable to change that condition.

This surrendering to sin is usually a gradual but escalating process. When you first commit a particular sin, you give the enemy a toehold in your life, so to speak. If you begin to consider that sin to be acceptable, the enemy gains a foothold. And if you unrepentantly repeat the same sin over and over, the enemy gains a stranglehold. In other words, you no longer control the sin. It controls you.

Practicing any kind of sin can lead to becoming a slave to that sin. But the Bible emphatically warns about specific categories of sins that are especially likely to lead to bondage. These include:

- Anger[95]
- Sexual immorality[96]
- Jealousy/envy[97]
- Greed[98]
- Idolatry[99]

The first four categories are fairly self-explanatory,[100] but idolatry is far less understood in today's culture, so let's discuss it.

Idolatry is serious. It breaks the first and second commandments[101] and God declared it to be appalling and shockingly evil.[102] Why? Because all idolatry disregards God and enthrones something else in his rightful place in our hearts. Our idols can be:

- Anything we depend on apart from God
- Anything we love more than God

While there can be a lot of overlap between these two

areas, they are nevertheless useful categories by which we should frequently examine ourselves.

Dependency. All addictions are idols, whether to alcohol, gambling, sex, drug abuse (legal or illegal), pornography, comfort, work, TV, sports, video games, eating, not eating, or anything else.

Love. An idol can also be anything we love or cherish more than God, whether girlfriend, boyfriend, husband, wife, children, parents, friendships, careers, money, possessions, pleasure, sleep, good looks, achievements, peer status, or even ministry.

When you "sacrifice" to an idol by over-committing your time, attention, affection, or resources to it, you become no different spiritually than idolatrous Jeshurun [Israel] who "sacrificed *to demons* that were no gods" (Deuteronomy 32:15–17; 1 Corinthians 10:20). Indeed, sacrificing even a part of your life to an idol makes you vulnerable to an enemy who wants to devour your entire life one bite at a time, an enemy who would love nothing better than for you to practice the sin of idolatry so much that you eventually become "of the devil."

Can an authentic Christian, one who has trusted in Christ alone for his or her personal sin dilemma, become "a slave to sin" and "of the devil"? Didn't Jesus also say, "If the Son sets you free, you will be free indeed"? (John 8:36). Yes, but the Bible also says, "For freedom Christ has set us free; *stand firm* therefore, and *do not submit* again to a yoke of slavery" (Galatians 5:1). Standing firm means:

- Actively resisting sin
- Deeply regretting sin
- Willfully repenting of sin

In other words, at a minimum "standing firm" means never waving the white flag. This approach to sin will be increasingly evident in those who are truly born again: "We know that everyone who has been born of God does not keep on sinning, but [Jesus Christ] who was born of God protects him, and the evil one does not touch him" (1 John 5:18).

If you are a real Christian, this verse should take your breath away—it means you can *never* be a slave of sin or the devil. But be careful, it also means that if you think of sin as acceptable, if you embrace it as part of your identity, you should definitely reconsider whether you are authentically born again or not. Be assured, "God's firm foundation stands, bearing this seal: 'The Lord knows those who are his,' and, 'Let everyone who names the name of the Lord depart from iniquity'" (2 Timothy 2:19).

Enemy Encampments: From the Occult to False Religions

For many, the Scriptures in this section will be simple review. For others, they will provide a timely warning. But for some, they will reveal the first steps toward freedom from being a spiritual prisoner of war. Let's begin here:

> When you come into the land that the LORD your God is giving you, you shall not learn to follow the *abominable practices* of those nations. *There shall not be found among you* anyone who burns his son or his daughter as an offering, anyone who practices *divination or tells fortunes or interprets omens, or a sorcerer or a charmer or a medium or a necromancer*

or one who inquires of the dead, for whoever does
these things is an abomination to the LORD . . . But as
for you, the LORD your God has not allowed you to
do this. (Deuteronomy 18:9–14)

God calls the practices listed in this passage *abomi-
nable* and he forbids you to participate in them because
they are satanic. Please do not immediately discount the
first one—burning one's son or daughter as an offering.
Child sacrifice still happens today, even literally. But more
often it happens where career and materialism are idolized
to such an extreme that relationships with children are
brutally sacrificed.

The passage specifically forbids your association with
the following kinds of people in any way that approves of
or actively participates in their false beliefs:

- Diviners: fortune tellers, astrologers, and psychics;
  including methods involving tarot cards, crystal balls,
  Ouija Boards, or palm reading
- Sorcerers: witches, warlocks, wizards
- Charmers: persons who put people under curses and
  spells
- Spirit mediums: persons who channel demons or
  dead humans through séances and other methods
- Necromancers: persons who conjure the dead in
  order to practice black magic

These activities are known as *occult* practices. In
Western culture, they are often considered to be either
vaguely "spiritual" (and therefore good), or else merely
interesting, harmless, fun, or entertaining. But they are *not*

good, and they are *not* harmless! Involving yourself in such activities can make you vulnerable to profound demonic influence. Do not dabble in them. Do not experiment with them. If these activities tempt you, turn and run!

> Do not be unequally yoked with unbelievers. For what partnership has righteousness with lawlessness? Or what fellowship has light with darkness? What accord has Christ with Belial? Or what portion does a believer share with an unbeliever? What agreement has the temple of God with idols? "*Therefore go out from their midst, and be separate from them,*" says the Lord, "and *touch no unclean thing*; then I will welcome you." (2 Corinthians 6:14–17)

The occult practitioners listed in the bullet points above knowingly or unknowingly worship Satan. No matter what they call it, they have placed their faith, hope, trust, and dependency in the evil one. They are members of the kingdom of darkness, not the kingdom of God. They practice spiritual idolatry. They are slaves of sin. They are of the devil. It is possible to build amicable relationships with them for purposes of evangelism, while still withholding approval of their practices and beliefs. Indeed, some Christians are called to do so. But this can be a tricky business that requires maturity, wisdom, and a clear sense of God's calling.[103]

These areas of false worship represent just a few of what we might call *enemy encampments*. Others include false religions such as Islam, Hinduism, and Buddhism, the neo-pagan religions, and a wide variety of pseudo-Christian cults and heresies.

How can you recognize a false religion, cult, or heresy when you encounter one? Start by determining the nature of its god:

- The God of the Bible is one God. Therefore polytheistic religions, like Hinduism and neo-paganism, are false.
- The God of the Bible is the triune God, consisting of three Persons, namely, Father, Son, and Holy Spirit. The god of Islam, Allah, is not triune—therefore Allah is not the one true God, and Islam is false.
- The God of the Bible sent God the Son to take on human flesh. Any religion that denies the simultaneous full divinity and full humanity of Jesus Christ is false.[104]

Other indicators of false religions, pseudo-Christian cults, and heresies include denying the Lordship of Christ,[105] enslaving people to human traditions,[106] distorting the gospel,[107] and offering guidance through any source that contravenes the absolute authority of the Bible, the written Word of God.[108]

Here are some things to avoid because the Bible never advocates them:

- Anything that involves emptying the mind, such as many of today's popular meditation and yoga techniques
- Anything that involves out-of-body experiences, non-medicinal drug use, sexual immorality, or physical extremes ranging from indulgence to asceticism
- Active participation in anything that requires

secret initiations, ceremonies, covenants, vows, promises, oaths, or pledges of a kind not approved in Scripture[109]

Many enemy encampments can seem to be good things, not at all occult or evil. Their leaders can be inspiring, and some may call themselves Christians. They may even use the Bible, taking God's words out of context and twisting their meaning, just like Satan did in the Garden of Eden and when he tempted Jesus in the wilderness. The New Testament presents explicit warnings on exactly this subject:

> For such men are false apostles, deceitful workmen, disguising themselves as apostles of Christ. And no wonder, for even Satan disguises himself as an angel of light. So it is no surprise if his servants, also, disguise themselves as servants of righteousness. Their end will correspond to their deeds. (2 Corinthians 11:13–15)

Involving yourself in a false religion, cult, or heresy can make you vulnerable to profound demonic influence. Don't go there. If you're tempted by it, flee.

Demonization: From Oppression to Possession

You might be surprised to learn that the same Greek word, *daimonizomai* (pronounced demon-is-oh-my) is translated in some English language Bibles to refer to both demon "oppression" and demon "possession" depending on the context.[110] But in fact, there is no biblical basis for making a distinction between these two. *Daimonizomai* is the verb form of *demon* and would best be translated "demonized" instead of "demon-oppressed" or "demon-possessed."

To be *demonized* means to be influenced by a demon. This influence can range from being hindered or harassed[111] to being overcome and controlled.

In a sense, the very idea of possession can be misleading, because nowhere does the Bible indicate that Satan can own a human. God owns everyone; Satan owns no one. Whether we are believer, unbeliever, Spirit-filled, or demonized, God owns us all.[112] He alone has the ultimate property rights to everyone, including those who will spend eternity away from his holy presence. Nothing in the Scriptures contradicts this truth. The concept of selling your soul to the devil is pure Hollywood. You are not your own to sell.

So while demons cannot *own* you, they can *control* you in varying degrees. They can demonize a person the way a puppeteer controls a puppet from the outside with a set of strings. In extreme cases, they can demonize a person the way a ventriloquist controls a dummy with his hand on the inside—they can control their body, convulse them, throw them to the ground, and use their tongue to vocalize.[113] Thus the Bible says a person "has a demon." When the demon is cast out, the hand of control is removed.

As we saw earlier in this chapter, demonization can come upon you because you essentially "asked for it" by practicing sin. But demonization can also come upon you when you've done nothing to invite it! The enemy can attack believers, even godly, obedient ones.

Job. For example, consider Job, a man who was "blameless and upright, one who feared God and turned away from evil" (Job 1:1). Satan systematically devastated his children, his wealth, and all his relationships. And when that wasn't enough, he "struck Job with loathsome sores from the sole of his foot to the crown of his head" (Job 2:7). It was a full frontal assault that God allowed. And when all was said and done, the outcome was a good one.[114]

Peter. The day before he went to the cross, Jesus told Peter, "Behold, Satan demanded to have you, that he might sift you like wheat." As best we can tell, Peter did nothing to invite this, but nevertheless Christ granted Satan permission. A spiritual attack took place and the enemy won that particular battle—Peter publicly denied the Lord three times. And yet, because Jesus prayed for him, Peter eventually turned and strengthened his brothers[115] and the outcome was very good. Upon the rock known as Peter, Christ built his church, and to this day the gates of hell have not prevailed against it, and never will.[116]

Paul. The apostle Paul was a man who had cast out demons. He had been given one of the most amazing privileges any man has ever received: he was "caught up to the third heaven" where he "heard things that cannot be told, which man may not utter." It was a revelation of "surpassing greatness." But afterwards, he was given a thorn *in* the flesh, "*a messenger of Satan*" to harass him. It was a messenger, not of God, but of Satan! As far as we know, Paul did not rebuke Satan, try to cast a demon out of his own body, or ask others to do so. And yet this, too, had a very, very good result. It enabled Paul to learn how to live in humility and joy that transcended his adverse circumstances:

> But [the Lord] said to me, "My grace is sufficient for you, for my power is made perfect in weakness." Therefore I will boast all the more gladly of my weaknesses, so that the power of Christ may rest upon me. For the sake of Christ, then, I am content with weaknesses, insults, hardships, persecutions, and calamities. For when I am weak, then I am strong. (2 Corinthians 12:1–10)

These three examples show that genuine Christians should never fear Satan. If God allows the evil one to assault you, he will always use it for your good and his glory.

What should you do if you or someone you know is demonized? We will answer that question in chapters seven and eight. But before we get there, let's take the next chapter to unveil the extremely good news I promised earlier.

Six

JESUS CHRIST, VICTORIOUS

Jesus stood up in the synagogue and read a prophecy that had been written hundreds of years before he was born:

> The Spirit of the Lord GOD is upon me,
> because the LORD has anointed me *to bring good*
> *news to the poor*; he has sent me *to bind up the bro-*
> *kenhearted, to proclaim liberty to the captives,*
> *and the opening of the prison to those who are bound;*
> to proclaim the year of the LORD's favor. (Isaiah
> 61:1–2b)

He then stopped, rolled up the scroll, gave it back to the attendant, and sat down. "And the eyes of all in the synagogue were fixed on him. And he began to say to them, '*Today this Scripture has been fulfilled in your hearing*'" (Luke 4:16–21).

The Hero had arrived.

There was never a question of the Son of God's superiority over the enemy. "For by him all things were created, *in heaven and on earth, visible and invisible, whether thrones or dominions or rulers or authorities*—all things were created through him and for him" (Colossians 1:16). He spun forth galaxies with a word. Could he not just as easily remove every rebel angel with a word as well? But that was not his plan. At least not yet.

Instead, Jesus came to set you free from sin and Satan by his victorious life, death, and resurrection. Next, we will look at each of these three bastions of Christ's triumph and their significance in your battle with the enemy.

Victorious Through His Life

Satan and demons sinned, fell to earth, and began tempting men and women long before the incarnation of the Son of God. But then one day, "when the fullness of time had come, God sent forth his Son, born of woman, born under the law, to redeem those who were under the law" (Galatians 4:4–5). In the gospel accounts, Christ's absolute supremacy over the enemy can be clearly seen. Satan never had the upper hand, not even for an instant.

Consider, for example, the forty-day battle with the devil that erupted in the wilderness when the Spirit led Jesus into temptation.[117] In each of Satan's three attempts, he twisted the Word of God to form a deception in hopes of triggering an ungodly desire in the Son of God. But the One sent to redeem those who were under the law responded by quoting truth from Deuteronomy, the Book of the Law. Unlike the first Adam, this last Adam, although truly tempted, never once yielded to that temptation—Jesus did not sin.

When the ordeal was over he said, "Be gone Satan," and the evil one immediately obeyed.[118] Then the same

Spirit that led Jesus into temptation led him away in power to his next destination.[119] It was a crucial victory for Jesus, and crucial good news for us.[120]

Christ was also victorious over demons, the devil's minions. Even by the thousands they were clearly no match for him.[121] Here is an example of a showdown between Jesus and a demon:

> And immediately there was in their synagogue a man with an unclean spirit. And he cried out, "What have you to do with us, Jesus of Nazareth? Have you come to destroy us? I know who you are—the Holy One of God." But Jesus rebuked him, saying, 'Be silent, and come out of him!' And the unclean spirit, convulsing him and crying out with a loud voice, came out of him. And they were all amazed, so that they questioned among themselves, saying, "What is this? A new teaching with authority! He commands even the unclean spirits, and they obey him." (Mark 1:23–27)

Here are three conclusions we can draw from this passage and similar ones found in Scripture:

- Demons openly acknowledged Jesus of Nazareth as the Messiah. They called him the Holy One of God,[122] the Son of God,[123] and the Son of the Most High God.[124]
- Ironically, although the hosts of darkness continually deceive, tempt, and accuse believers in an all-out effort to destroy their faith, they themselves are never agnostics—they *believe* and they *shudder*.[125]
- Demons never dared to denounce Christ to his face.

In fact, they obeyed his commands instantly, a clear indication of Christ's total superiority over the enemy.

If you ever have reservations about engaging in spiritual warfare, remember why Jesus came: "The reason the Son of God appeared was to *destroy* the works of the devil" (1 John 3:8).[126] This is good news! This is inspiring! It should embolden you to put on the full armor of God and enter the fray every day.

God the Son took on flesh and blood in order to dismantle and demolish the kingdom of darkness. He said, "I have come into the world as light, so that whoever believes in me may *not remain in darkness*" (John 12:46). Jesus Christ *is* "the light of the world" (John 8:12). "The light shines in the darkness, and *the darkness has not overcome it*" (John 1:5). Jesus defeats the darkness; the darkness does not defeat him. This is extremely good news for those who are called to follow him into the darkness to engage in battle.

During his victorious life on earth, Jesus cast out demons "by the finger of God" (Luke 11:20). He entered the strong man's house, bound him, and plundered his "goods"[127] by setting Satan's captives free.

Victorious Through His Death

But the day would arrive when, by all appearances, Satan was the strong man and Jesus was bound—no, nailed—to a cross of wood. At Calvary, the evil one came and plundered the King of the kingdom of God.

Or did he?

Imagine you are a disciple of Jesus, walking alongside him as he enters Jerusalem on Palm Sunday. The sun is shining, the crowds are ecstatic, and it seems that all your hopes and dreams are beginning to come true. But before you have a chance to bask in the glow, you hear Jesus say, "I will no longer talk much with you, for *the ruler of this world* is coming. He has no claim on me" (John 14:30). Confusion immediately sets in, but one thing is clear: Jesus is saying that this ruler is Satan, and he is getting nearer.

Tensions mount throughout the week until, on Thursday night, the unthinkable happens. The satanically inspired Judas Iscariot arrives with the kiss of death, leading a mob armed with swords and clubs. Jesus looks them all in the eye and says, "This is *your hour*, and *the power of darkness*" (Luke 22:3, 47–53).

As you and your friends scatter frantically into the woods, the words *your hour* ring over and over in your thoughts. Suddenly the mysterious exchange you heard earlier in the week comes rushing into your mind:

> "Now is my soul troubled" [said Jesus]. "And what shall I say? 'Father, save me from *this hour*'? But for this purpose I have come to *this hour*. Father, glorify your name." Then a voice came from heaven: "I have glorified it, and I will glorify it again." The crowd that stood there and heard it said that it had thundered. Others said, "An angel has spoken to him." Jesus answered, "This voice has come for your sake, not mine. Now is the judgment of this world; *now will the ruler of this world be cast out. And I, when I am lifted up from the earth, will draw all people to myself.*" (John 12:27–32)

It took a while for the disciples to understand that the hour of the power of darkness was also the hour of Christ's glory. Only the most glorious Person in the universe could accomplish what Jesus had done during that hour. By being lifted up from the earth to die, he caused God to cancel "the record of debt that stood against us with its legal demands. This he set aside, nailing it to the cross. *He disarmed the rulers and authorities and put them to open shame, by triumphing over them in him*" (Colossians 2:14–15).

- Satanic rulers and authorities? *Disarmed* and forever disgraced.
- The ruler of this world? *Cast out*, for the true King has been lifted up.
- The strong man? *Bound* by him who is infinitely stronger.

When you feel afraid of the enemy and his power, these may be the most encouraging words in the entire Bible: "Since therefore the children share in flesh and blood, he himself likewise partook of the same things, that through death he might destroy the one who has the power of death, that is, the devil, and deliver all those who through fear of death were subject to lifelong slavery" (Hebrews 2:14–15).

So we need one more bullet point:

- The devil with the power of death? *Destroyed*, and his slaves delivered to freedom.

Ironically, the weapon God used to defeat Satan was Jesus' own death. This resulted in a crown of glory for

Christ and, for us, what theologians call *substitutionary atonement.* Notice the idea in this amazing verse, "But we see him who for a little while was made lower than the angels, namely Jesus, crowned with glory and honor because of the suffering of death, so that by the grace of God *he might taste death for everyone*" (Hebrews 2:9).

This "tasting death" that Jesus accomplished on behalf of others is at the heart of substitutionary atonement. It's an essential concept, so let's break it down a little:

- *Substitution*: an act performed in your place by a qualified representative (in this case, Christ)
- *Atonement*: the price paid to reconcile two parties (in this case, you and God) who are at odds over an offense (your Satan-like rebellion against God)
- *Substitutionary Atonement*: the price paid *by* Christ that was due *from* you (your death) by offering up *for* you his own infinitely valuable life as a substitute

As we engage in spiritual warfare, may the precious phrase *substitutionary atonement* be always on our minds, in our hearts, and at the tip of our tongues. In these two words we can see and savor the victory of Christ's death that has been irrevocably and forever applied to our lives.

Victorious Through His Resurrection

Mary Magdalene knew what it was like to be controlled by demons, and she knew what it was like to have Jesus cast them all out. She also knew what it was like to stand near the cross and watch Jesus die (John 19:25). All these events were shocking, but what awaited her on the third day was beyond anyone's imagination: "Now when [Jesus] rose early on the first day of the week, *he appeared first to Mary Magdalene,* from whom he had cast out seven demons" (Mark 16:9).

How ironic it is that the first person to see the risen Christ was a woman who had previously been mastered by the enemy seven-fold. Why was Mary Magdalene, of all people, given the extraordinary blessing of being the first to see the Son of God in his resurrected, physical body? Is it possible God was emphasizing the centrality of Jesus' role as the one who can both free and redeem even those most severely under Satan's sway?

Mary Magdalene was the first to see the risen Lord, but hundreds more would soon follow. "He presented himself alive to them after his suffering by many proofs, appearing to them during forty days and speaking about the kingdom of God" (Acts 1:3).[128] The following two passages reveal the glorious victory of this resurrected Christ: "God raised him up, loosing the pangs of death, because it was *not possible* for him to be held by it" (Acts 2:24). "We know that Christ, being raised from the dead, will never die again; *death no longer has dominion over him*" (Romans 6:9).

Jesus has totally and permanently conquered death. His claim to be the resurrection and the life[129] turned out to be true after all. Here are some of the implications of this historical fact:

- He really is who he said he was. He was "declared to be the Son of God in power according to the Spirit of holiness by his resurrection from the dead, Jesus Christ our Lord" (Romans 1:4). Identity confirmed!

- The devil no longer holds the power of death, Christ does. Jesus said, "I died, and behold I am alive forevermore, and *I have the keys of Death and Hades*" (Revelation 1:18). Security established!
- If you are united to Christ by authentic faith, his promise is true for you: "Because I live you also will live" (John 14:19). Eternally comforting!
- If you are "in Christ" you are already "raised… up with him and seated… with him in the heavenly places" (Ephesians 2:6). Utterly astonishing!

If the death of Christ is the wellspring of the good news, the resurrection is its mighty fountain. Can it get any better? Yes! God the Father,

Raised [Christ] from the dead and seated him at his right hand in the heavenly places, *far above all rule and authority and power and* dominion, and above every name that is named, *not only in this age but also in the one to come*. And he *put all things under his* feet and gave him as head over all things to the church, which is his body, the fullness of him who fills all in all. (Ephesians 1:20–23)

Christ ascended to the right hand of the majesty on high where he reigns at this very moment! "For to this end Christ died and lived again, that he might be Lord both of the dead and of the living" (Romans 14:9). In fact no human, dead or alive, and no angel, holy or fallen, escapes his command:

[Christ] humbled himself by becoming obedient to

the point of death, even death on a cross. Therefore God has highly exalted him and bestowed on him the name that is above every name, so that at the name of Jesus *every knee* should bow, *in heaven and on earth and under the earth*, and *every tongue* confess that Jesus Christ is Lord, to the glory of God the Father." (Philippians 2:8–11)

Are you willing in the here and now to bow the knee to the risen Jesus Christ, the Lord who reigns? If you are, then the flow from the fountain is a mighty torrent carrying you into the Savior's open arms, and not even Satan can stop it.

Who is to condemn? Christ Jesus is the one who *died*—more than that, who *was raised*—who *is at the right hand of God*, who indeed is interceding for us .. .. For I am sure that neither death nor life, *nor angels nor rulers*, nor things present nor things to come, *nor powers*, nor height nor depth, nor anything else in all creation, will be able to separate us from the love of God in Christ Jesus our Lord." (Romans 8:34, 38–39)

The good news about Satan? He's already been utterly defeated by the life, death, resurrection, and reign of Jesus Christ. And all the powers of the kingdom of darkness combined can never, under *any* circumstances, snatch you out of his mighty, tender hand.[130]

But the enemy has not yet admitted defeat, and serious battles must be fought each and every day. Please read the following "how to" chapters of this book with the victorious Christ continuously in mind. He makes all the difference in spiritual warfare.

Seven

HOW TO RESIST THE DEVIL

The Bible uses a single, uncomplicated word to tell you how to respond when the enemy attacks: *resist*. When you do, the promised result is astonishing: the devil will flee from you.[131] He will flee!

This, too, is good news about Satan.

In this sense, spiritual warfare simply comes down to knowing how to resist. So who do you need to *be*, and what do you need to *do*, to make the enemy tuck tail and retreat from your presence? These are the questions we will address in this chapter.

Remember Your Identity in Christ

If you are united to Christ by authentic faith you *already are* everything you need to be in order to resist the enemy. But it is easy to lose sight of this when you are in the heat of the battle. So it's vital to maintain your focus by continually recalling:

- Who you are

- Whose you are
- Who you are with

Who are you? In Christ you are a new creation with a new identity.[132] You are an adopted member of God's family.[133] You are a citizen of heaven.[134] And you're a personal friend of the Son of God.[135] Astonishing!

Whose are you? You "have died to the law through the body of Christ, so that you may *belong* to another, to him who has been raised from the dead" (Romans 7:4). If you are in Christ, you are his.

Who are you with? God made you alive together *with* Christ ... and raised you up *with* him and seated you *with* him in the heavenly places in Christ Jesus.[136] If you are in Christ, you are with him every moment.

Many books on spiritual warfare tell you to declare your identity out loud before the hosts of darkness. Although this method is not found in the Bible, if it helps you to *remind yourself* of who you are in Christ, and if you can *encourage others* by declaring this good news, then shout it from the rooftops:

> Christ is my Redeemer,
> I am a captive he set free.
> Christ is my Protector, my Savior, my Treasure,
> I am in him, and he is in me.

In spiritual warfare, it is vital at all times to remember who you are. But it is equally important to remember who you aren't:

- You are not the victorious one, Christ is.[137]

- You are not the one with all authority, Christ is.[138]
- You are not the one who delivers people, Christ is.[139]

Now here's the good news about these truths: if the victorious one has exercised his authority to set you free, then his victory is your victory! No wonder an exuberant Paul proclaimed, "Thanks be to God, who in Christ always leads us in triumphal procession" (2 Corinthians 2:14). We don't fight *for* victory, we fight *from* victory— his!

When you consider Satan's arsenal of weapons, only one of them can ultimately destroy you: his accusation that the debt for your sins has not been fully paid. But if you are in Christ, the record of debt that stood against you with its legal demands was set aside![140] So today Satan can harass you, and at times he will. He can hinder you, and at times succeed. But Satan can never damn you. Why? Because the sin-atoning death of Christ has been irrevocably applied to you!

Many books on spiritual warfare tell you to proclaim the cross or the blood of Christ out loud before the hosts of darkness. Again, there are no examples in Scripture where demons are confronted in this manner, and we are not told to follow this practice. Nevertheless, if it helps you to *remind yourself* of the connection between Christ's death and your life, and if you can *encourage others* by declaring this good news, then shout it out:

> Far be it from me to boast
> except in *the cross* of our Lord Jesus Christ,
> by which the world has been crucified to me,
> and I to the world. (Galatians 6:14)

Who do you need to be to make the enemy tuck tail and retreat from your presence? If you are united by authentic faith to "Jesus Christ and him crucified" (1 Corinthians 2:2), *you already are that person*. You are ready, right now, to do what it takes to resist the enemy.

Put on the Armor

The entire Bible provides God-breathed insights and instructions for spiritual warfare.[141] But the specific methods, strategies, and tactics we need for resisting the enemy today are most clearly set forth in the letters written to the first century churches: Romans through Revelation. Why? Because, just like us, those believers lived after the death, resurrection, and ascension of Christ, and after the arrival of the Holy Spirit. And just like us, they lived within fierce spiritual war zones where they were subject to Satan's deceptions, temptations, accusations, allies, and maneuvers.

Ephesians 6:10–18 provides the most detailed how-to on spiritual warfare in the entire Bible. These extremely helpful verses are worthy of your careful attention— both for what they say, and what they don't say. In this passage, Paul tells the Ephesians at length how to face off against the nonmaterial demonic beings with whom they struggled. Yet he never even hints at rebuking, binding, loosing, calling down, or casting out these evil spirits. Instead, he reveals the core strategy for spiritual warfare by repeatedly emphasizing a single, uncomplicated word: stand. "Put on the whole armor of God, that you may be able to *stand* against the schemes of the devil . . . Therefore take up the whole armor of God, that you may be able to *withstand* in the evil day, and having done all, to *stand* firm. *Stand* therefore ..." (Ephesians 6:11–14).

The repetition is there to make the command impossible to miss: the Ephesians must never back down. How could they stand firm against such a formidable foe? By being "strong in the Lord and in the strength of his might" (v 10). In other words, when the power to engage the enemy comes from Christ (not human willpower), it makes all the difference. In fact, it guarantees a positive outcome.

Paul's letter to the Ephesians is primarily about the meaning and application of the gospel. Finding the six components of the "armor of God" (vv 14–17) at the end of that letter would have indicated to the original readers that this armor is ours as a direct result of the completed and ongoing work of Christ. Therefore, to correctly understand and utilize the armor, you and I need to take a gospel-centered approach.

Here's how to rightly utilize each component of the armor of God.

The belt of truth. Fasten on the true doctrine of Jesus—the good news about who he actually is and what he really did—and oppose all the lies the enemy promotes about him, that is, "every lofty opinion raised against the knowledge of God" (2 Corinthians 10:5).

Are you tempted to believe in a Jesus of your own making, one who is not the precise Jesus of the Bible? Do you sometimes gravitate to the popular, man-centered views of Christianity? This is spiritual warfare. Resist!

The breastplate of righteousness. Put on the righteousness that is credited to those who are united to Christ by authentic faith.[142] Embrace the practice of walking in obedience out of gratitude for purchased grace.

Are you tempted to credit your right standing

before God to your personal law-keeping?[143] Or do you sometimes feel compelled to "continue in sin that grace may abound"(Romans 6:1)? This, too, is spiritual warfare. Stand firm!

The shoes of readiness given by the gospel of peace. Plant your feet exclusively on the good news about the peace we enjoy with God as a result of who Christ is and what he has done. And always be ready to share the news with others.[144]

Are you tempted to disregard the gospel and stand on other kinds of "good" news instead? Do you sometimes experience the urge to withhold the gospel from people far and near who need to hear it? This, too, is spiritual warfare. Resist!

The shield of faith. Stand behind the good news of Christ's death as the God-ordained solution to your personal sin dilemma. His death completely removed your guilt, condemnation, shame, curse, and eternal punishment.

Are you tempted to put your faith in things other than Christ's death in order to make you right with God? Do you sometimes struggle to believe his death is truly all-sufficient for you? This, too, is spiritual warfare. Stand firm!

The helmet of salvation. Protect your mind with a clear understanding of the way salvation works according to the only reliable source, the Bible. The Five Solas[145] summarize the life-changing, mighty, vital doctrines of the good news. We are saved unto God, saved from our sins, and saved out of the clutches of the enemy:

- By grace alone (Sola Gratia)

- Through faith alone (Sola Fide)
- Based on the person and work of Christ alone (Solus Christus)
- Revealed in the Bible alone (Sola Scriptura)
- To the glory of God alone (Soli Deo Gloria)

Are you tempted to doubt that a sinner like you can truly be saved? Do you sometimes battle with fears of eternal condemnation? This, too, is spiritual warfare. Resist!

The sword of the Spirit. The Bible is *the sword of the Spirit* because it was breathed out by God the Holy Spirit and is therefore living and active, absolutely authoritative, and utterly unlike any other book.[146] From cover to cover it reveals the good news of the redemption of fallen mankind through the Person and finished work of Jesus Christ.

Are you tempted to disregard Scriptures that conflict with your personal views or lifestyle? Do you sometimes dispute the Bible in order to make room for your ongoing disobedience? This, too, is spiritual warfare. Stand firm!

Finally, how do you "put on" these six components of armor? By "praying at all times in the Spirit, with all prayer and supplication" (Ephesians 6:18). In other words, *continually pray them on*, piece-by-piece, by asking the Spirit to firmly apply the gospel to every aspect of your life every day. Put on the whole armor of God like this, and you will stand, not fall, in spiritual warfare. Why will you stand? Because of who Jesus is, and what he has already done to defeat the enemy.

What do you need to *do* to resist the enemy in addition to armoring up? Don't miss the two techniques described next. They are equally essential.

Two Paradoxical Methods of Resistance

Look carefully at the context of "resist the devil and he will flee from you" and you will quickly discover two crucial methods for getting your spiritual foe to flee. Ironically, both of them make you seem weak, not strong.

Humbly Submit to God

The Bible makes it clear that being weak in yourself before God's power and glory produces spiritual strength. James puts it this way: "God opposes the proud, but gives grace to the humble. Submit yourselves therefore to God…. Humble yourselves before the Lord, and he will exalt you" (James 4:6–7, 10).

The first point carries a vital message: the pride of self-reliance is only going to work against you when it comes to resisting the devil. In fact, it will cause *God* to work against you!

In the context of spiritual warfare, humility is the simple act of recognizing that in yourself you are no match for the temptations served up by the devil and his demons, aided by the world and the flesh. It's admitting you are totally dependent on God's enabling power in order to resist. When you humble yourself in this manner, James promises that two astonishing things will happen in God's perfect timing: grace will flow, and God will exalt you above the temptation. Humbly submit to the Lord, fight Satan God's way, and grace and exaltation are yours.

This is precisely what happened with Paul. He suffered an ongoing, bodily, spiritual attack, a thorn in the flesh to keep him from becoming conceited. He knew how to cast out demons and yet did not perform self-deliverance. Instead, he asked God to remove the thorn and was told, "My grace is sufficient for you." Paul humbly submitted and replied, "When I am weak, then I am strong" (2 Corinthians 12:9–10).

This is precisely what happened with Jesus, too.[147] The night before he went to the cross, he humbly submitted to the Father, saying, "Not my will, but yours, be done" (Luke 22:42). Then, faced with Satan's assault in the ultimate spiritual battle of the ages, Jesus did not call down legions of angels to defend himself.[148] Instead, he humbled himself to the point of death, even death on a cross.[149] The good news dawned on the third day, and the brilliance of his exaltation has been unstoppable ever since.[150]

Pride is natural to all humans and fallen angels. Clothe yourself in humility and you will surprise everyone, including yourself. Then lift your eyes and watch the enemy flee.

Confess Sin and Repent

It is no coincidence that the passage from James we just looked at appears in a chapter about sin. In order to stop sin from interfering with your ability to resist the enemy, you are commanded to "cleanse your hands, you sinners, and purify your hearts, you double-minded" (James 4:8).

In other words, confess your sins. Openly acknowledge your unclean hands (sinful actions), your impure heart (sinful desires), and your hypocritical way of thinking (sinful mind). Confess your sins, one at a time, agreeing with God about their utter sinfulness. Finally, "submit yourself to God" by turning away from them, solidly renouncing them, and refusing to look back at them. In other words, *repent*!

Repentance from known sin is not optional in spiritual warfare. You can't give opportunity to the devil[151] and make him flee from you at the same time. But let's be honest. All of us at times find ourselves cherishing and protecting certain kinds of sin. We may *want to want* to repent, but deep down we struggle to surrender the sin and submit to God. At times like these, Paul's words describe us perfectly, "I have the desire to do what is right, but not the ability to carry it out. For I do not do the good I want, but the evil I do not want is what I keep on doing" (Romans 7:18–19).

What are we to do? At the height of Paul's despair he revealed the key word, "Wretched man that I am! Who will *deliver* me from this body of death?" The answer? Jesus will (Romans 7:24–25).

Jesus Christ "gave himself for our sins to *deliver* us from the present evil age, according to the will of our God and Father" (Galatians 1:4). So when you feel stuck in sin, ask him—no, *plead* with him—to deliver you from it.

And there's one more thing you can do. You can ask God to *grant* you repentance. "God may perhaps grant [you] repentance leading to a knowledge of the truth, and [you] may come to [your] senses and *escape from the snare of the devil*, after being captured by him to do his will" (2 Timothy 2:25–26).

Yes, repentance is a gift. Ask God to grant it to you. All that stuff you don't actually want to stop doing, but you know is harming you and leading you down the enemy's path? Cry out for the gift of repentance, even if—*especially if*—you don't feel like repenting. Persist in prayer for it. Don't quit until the gift arrives. Because until repentance materializes, you will remain in the devil's trap, unable and unwilling to resist him.

As you continually confess your sins and continually repent, continually lift your eyes and "draw near to God, and he will draw near to you" (James 4:8). What grace for sinners! What good news! Bask in the joy of restored communion with the triune God, and it won't be long before the devil heads for the hills.

How paradoxical! One would think the best way to deal with a spiritual enemy would be to flex your spiritual muscles and start pushing evil spirits around. But Paul did not do that when he was attacked. Neither did Jesus. And neither should you—at least not as your primary strategy. Instead, remember who you are, armor up, get humble, and submit to God by dealing with your sins.

Responding to an Attack

In spiritual warfare, you will experience frequent minor skirmishes, a flaming dart here and there. But there will also be times when you feel like the enemy has you surrounded and will not relent until you wave the white flag. What should you do?

First, make sure you have applied everything in this chapter. Then remember Satan's limitations, and that because of these limitations you are ultimately dealing with God, not the enemy. Next, pray and clearly express your dependency on God. Ask him to "deliver you from the evil one,"[152] and (as applicable) to remove the thorn, all the while maintaining the attitude of Christ at Gethsemane, who prayed to his Father, "nevertheless, not as I will, but as you will" (Matthew 26:39). After that, cling to his promises, like the ones in Psalm 121:

I lift up my eyes to the hills.
From where does my help come?
My help comes from the LORD,
who made heaven and earth.

He will not let your foot be moved;
he who keeps you will not slumber.
Behold, he who keeps Israel
will neither slumber nor sleep.

The LORD is your keeper;
the LORD is your shade on your right hand.
The sun shall not strike you by day,
nor the moon by night.

The LORD will keep you from all evil;
he will keep your life.
The LORD will keep
your going out and your coming in
from this time forth and forevermore.

Are you frightened? Trust him. Are you dying? Trust him. Is spiritual warfare raging all around you? Trust God. Trust him. Trust him. Trust him.

He is your all-powerful, all-knowing God who demonstrated his love for you in the giving of the unspeakable gift, his Son, on the cross.

He can be trusted!

And while you're trusting, never forget you are a member of the glorious kingdom of God, so always be willing to seek help from your community of true believers, including perhaps a pastor or counselor. In some cases it may also be helpful to see a medical doctor. Because of the local church, on the human level you need never be alone in your battle. Moreover, seeking help from others is itself a means of humbling yourself before God, as you trust him enough to take advantage of the built-in help he has afforded you in the local church.

All the while, keep the victorious Savior directly in your sights. Sooner or later, one way or another, you will become aware that he always leads you in triumphal procession. Sometimes this is hard to see…but he always has, and always will.

So never, ever stop resisting. It's a promise of the living God and it couldn't be more certain if his finger wrote it on a tablet of stone:

Resist the devil, and he *will* flee from you.

Eight
HOW TO HELP
THE DEMONIZED

Satan and demons are real. They continuously and aggressively engage in spiritual warfare, and they certainly don't lose every battle. As a result, many people today are demonized on various levels.

Can you help them? If so, how?

The apostles often helped by ordering a demon to leave. For example, Paul encountered a slave girl who "had a spirit of divination." He simply said to the spirit, "'I command you in the name of Jesus Christ to come out of her.' And it came out that very hour" (Acts 16:16–18).

- Does God intend for us to help the demonized the same way Paul and the other apostles did?
- Are today's believers authorized and called to confront demons directly?
- Are we commanded to do so?
- If so, is this the primary way we should extend help to those who are under demonic influence or control?

These are the questions we will address in this chapter.

The Authority to Cast Out Demons?

During his earthly ministry, Jesus Christ demonstrated absolute power over demons. He endowed his immediate disciples with authority to cast out demons in his name, and they did so.[153] This authority was later extended to a broader circle of seventy-two disciples.[154] After the resurrection, others including Paul were added to the list.

The question is, are we on the list, too? To keep it simple, let's put it this way: have we been given by Jesus the *authority* to cast out demons?

Let's quickly revisit what we mean by "casting out" a demon. In chapter 5, we saw that if people actively open themselves up to demonic influence, demons can come to control them in varying degrees. In extreme cases, the demons can act almost like a ventriloquist with a dummy, controlling their body as well as their voice and emotional expressions.[155] When that hand of control is removed against the demon's will, we say the demon has been cast out.

Today, there are differing opinions on whether Christians have the kind of God-given authority we're talking about. Many Christians around the world claim to cast out demons, and some are apparently able to. But since even non-Christians can sometimes cast out demons,[156] this doesn't actually answer our question. Remember the premise of this book: we don't want to draw any conclusions that don't follow readily from Scripture. So the question we're asking right now is whether *the Bible* indicates that Christians alive today have the authority and calling to cast out demons.

Four books of the Bible mention the practice of casting

out demons: Matthew, Mark, Luke, and Acts. The silence of the other 62 books—especially the 22 of them that follow Acts—is significant. But regardless, does anything in those four books instill us with confidence that we, too, are endowed with this kind of God-given authority?

Mark's rendition of the Great Commission is the only passage that directly connects the dots between today's believers and the authority to cast out demons. In it, Jesus told the disciples, "Go into all the world and proclaim the gospel to the whole creation. Whoever believes and is baptized will be saved, but whoever does not believe will be condemned. And these signs will accompany *those who believe: in my name they will cast out demons . . .*" (Mark 16:15–17).[157]

One might paraphrase this as follows, "You will know the ones who are genuinely saved by faith because they will have the ability to cast out demons in my name." But a question arises in the next verse when Jesus adds, "they will speak in new tongues; they will pick up serpents with their hands; and if they drink any deadly poison, it will not hurt them; they will lay their hands on the sick, and they will recover" (Mark 16:18).

If verse 17 applies to all genuine believers today, then so does verse 18. If you are not quite sure what to make of this, rest assured, you're not alone. Christians have debated about verse 18 for centuries. The controversy will not be settled here. However, most scholars agree that no single passage of Scripture—without the support of others—should be used as a proof text to support a doctrine. This principle would lead us to conclude that *Mark 16:15–18 does not establish biblical support for the idea that today's Christians are endowed with authority to cast out demons.*

Furthermore, as mentioned earlier, the Scripture below shows that the ability to cast out demons does *not* necessarily prove a person is saved. Jesus said, "On that day many will say to me, 'Lord, Lord, did we not prophesy in your name, and *cast out demons in your name*, and do many mighty works in your name?' And then will I declare to them, '*I never knew you; depart from me*, you workers of lawlessness'" (Matthew 7:22–23).

Jesus did not dispute their claim of authentically casting out demons—but he did essentially cast *them* out by commanding them to depart from him. Why? Because they were not authentically saved.

We have seen that there's one New Testament passage addressing the issue of present-day Christians and the authority to cast out demons, but it is too isolated and unclear to build a doctrine on. So let's consider the idea of authority in general. After all, Colossians 2:9–10 says, "For in [Christ] the whole fullness of deity dwells bodily, and *you* have been filled *in him*, who is the head of all rule and *authority*." In other words, based on our union with Christ, his authority has become our authority.

Without a doubt, this means Christians today have a *lot* of authority. But are there any limits on it? Any conditions? Of course—there must be some, since any authority we are given will always be subject to Christ's, and therefore cannot be precisely equal to it.[158] (That is, becoming a Christian doesn't mean you are or ever will be on the same level with Jesus!) And that brings us back to our original question: does our authority *specifically include* the authority to cast out demons? If it does, it's not found in this passage.

At the end of our search, the Bible doesn't clearly and

directly say that today's believers are endowed with the authority to cast out demons.

But it doesn't clearly and directly say we aren't.

A Command to Cast Out Demons?

There is still another question well worth asking—are we *commanded* in Scripture to cast out demons? This is vital because we can be confident that God would not *command* us to do something without *authorizing* us to do it.

The original twelve disciples were definitely given such a command. When Jesus called the twelve and "gave them authority over unclean spirits, to cast them out," three sentences later he added, "Heal the sick, raise the dead, cleanse lepers, *cast out demons*" (Matthew 10:1, 8). The disciples were given authority *and* command.[159] The seventy-two were also given authority, and while Jesus approved of them using it, the *command* to do so was apparently not part of his charge to them.[160]

We have already established that you can't say from Scripture that we have explicitly been given the *authority* to cast out demons. So, does the *command* to cast out demons that Jesus gave to the twelve automatically extend to us? If not, does some other passage give us any kind of similar command?

Matthew's rendition of the Great Commission, given to the eleven remaining disciples, possibly speaks to this question: "Go therefore and make disciples of all nations, baptizing *them* in the name of the Father and of the Son and of the Holy Spirit, teaching *them* to observe *all* that I have *commanded you*. And behold, I am with you always, to the end of the age'" (Matthew 28:19–20).

In the context of our discussion, one might be inclined to paraphrase this passage as follows: "You eleven go and make disciples everywhere, and when you do, teach them to do everything that I commanded you to do—including my commandment to cast out demons." The passage doesn't say that, but some might argue it implies that. But if that was part of what Jesus intended to communicate, we have to ask why none of the New Testament letters pass along that emphasis to the churches.

Many of those letters were written by men to whom Jesus personally gave the Great Commission. And even though Paul, apostle to the Gentiles, himself had experience with casting out demons, there is not one word in his letters about the subject.

Similarly, in Revelation chapters 2 and 3, the risen and ascended Christ is speaking to seven New Testament churches. (Please consider taking just a few minutes now to read those two chapters carefully.)

Notice that all of these churches were located in intense spiritual war zones. When Jesus addressed the churches in Smyrna and Philadelphia he referred to a "synagogue of Satan" (Revelation 2:9). He said to the church in Pergamum, "I know where you dwell, where Satan's throne is" (Revelation 2:13). And he indicated that some in the church in Thyatira had learned "what some call the deep things of Satan" (Revelation 2:24).

Yet, just like Paul's letters and the other epistles, there is no instruction or direction whatsoever about the casting out of demons. Instead, Jesus emphasized the following:

- Turn from sin and pursue holy living.
- Turn from false teaching and cling to the truth.

- Have faith in Christ and treasure him as your first love.
- Persevere under adversity.

So at the end of this search, we must conclude that *no reliable statement in Scripture authorizes or commands Christians alive today to cast out demons*. But we must also conclude with equal force that nothing in Scripture *forbids us* from casting out demons. In fact, here is a passage showing the extent to which Jesus did not prohibit the practice: "John said to him, 'Teacher, we saw someone casting out demons in your name, and we tried to stop him, because he was not following us.' But Jesus said, '*Do not stop him*, for no one who does a mighty work in my name will be able soon afterward to speak evil of me.'" (Mark 9:38–39)

There's also one more concept to consider: gifting. Some believers *are* specially gifted with the ability to discern the spirits, and these are certainly called to exercise their gift.[161] From time to time, Christians possessing this gift may encounter those who are profoundly demonized. In each case, such people must seek God's leading for how he would have them use that gift of discernment.

So where does all this leave us?

Biblical Help for the Demonized

If the Bible neither commands nor forbids Christians alive today to cast out demons, and if the practice of doing so is essentially absent from all the New Testament epistles, it does seem like we're on solid biblical footing to conclude that God does not expect the casting out of demons to be a common, standard part of the believer's responsibility. What, then, *is* our responsibility? How are you and I, as regular Christians, supposed to engage in spiritual warfare on behalf of those, whether Christian or not, who lie under Satan's sway?

As noted previously in this book, and in light of everything we learned about the enemy in the first five chapters, I believe we can summarize the enemy's mission for the demonized in four initiatives:

- To prevent or destroy their faith in God and the gospel
- To enslave or ensnare them in sinful rebellion
- To get them to submit control of their mind, will, body, and emotions
- To commandeer any glory God would ever get from their life

The Bible declares emphatically that *all* believers are to call *all* people, including the demonized, to repent, place their faith in Jesus Christ, and then glorify God with their lives. These four initiatives, which are diametrically opposed to the enemy's, form a framework by which we can ready ourselves for a truly biblical approach to spiritual warfare.

Preparations

The first two initiatives involve getting prepared to help the demonized:

Prepare for battle. You never know who or what you are going to encounter on any given day. Here are three ways to get ready:

1. Regularly memorize key Scriptures so they will be on the tip of your tongue when you need them.[162] Examples are included in Appendix 2.
2. Regularly confess your sins, and repent from them as described earlier. Examine your life in light of God's Word, and if needed, ask him to grant repentance.
3. Regularly "pray on" the full armor of God as described in chapter 7, especially remembering your need to "be strong *in the Lord* and in the strength of *his* might."[163]

Diligently practicing these three spiritual disciplines can help you become and remain humbly submitted to God—and make you more ready, willing, and able to be used by him to provide timely help to those in need.

Provide prayer. Before moving forward to help someone, when possible, spend time in prayer and enlist the prayers of others. Pray for:

1. The wisdom to know when to speak and when to listen
2. The Spirit of God to illuminate the Word of God
3. The Spirit and the Son to intercede for all involved
4. The enabling power and protection of the Holy Spirit
5. A spirit of gentleness, and that you will not be tempted yourself[164]

Modeling a spontaneous prayer along the lines of the Lord's Prayer is also an excellent approach. Perhaps something like this: "May your name be hallowed, your will be done, and your kingdom come in this person's life. May forgiveness be received and given. May you not allow them to be put to the test, but instead, may you deliver them from evil and the evil one. And may all the glory go to you, the one who alone is worthy of glory."

Opportunities often occur spontaneously. In those cases, the one-word prayer, "Help!" has significance, since it lets both you and the Lord know where your dependency is anchored.

Tactics

The following tactics go head-to-head with the four initiatives of the enemy's mission, and they do this by emphasizing faith, sin, submission, and glory. When these tactics succeed, they cause real casualties to the enemy. Casting out a demon accomplishes little unless these tactics are also diligently applied:

Identify lies. Deception is involved in every enemy attack. Probe for lies and half-truths by using strategic, open-ended questions such as:

- How would you describe what is bothering you?
- Whom do you believe is responsible?
- How did you get into this situation?
- What do you believe would make you feel better?
- How can you justify your thinking about this?
- Who or what are you relying on in this situation?
- What do you believe God's role is in this?

Listen very carefully to the answers given to these questions. Weigh everything you hear against everything you know in Scripture. In particular, try to detect lies about the nature of God and anything that contradicts the Five Solas mentioned in chapter seven. When you identify a deception, gently offer correction using the Bible. If the person agrees with you, ask him or her to specifically renounce each lie in prayer to God.

Whenever the truth prevails, give glory together to the triune God!

Identify sins. The Bible commands us to *expose* the unfruitful works of darkness[165] and call sinners—both believers and unbelievers—to repentance.[166] This also involves strategic questioning and careful listening:

- Which sins do you seem unable to stop committing?
- Which commands in the Bible are the ones you just cannot agree with?
- Who or what could you not imagine living without?
- What aspect of your life do you wish you could hide from the Lord?
- What do you obsess over?
- Do you struggle with anger, sexual immorality, jealousy/envy, greed, and/or idolatry?
- Do you have any present or past active, approving participation in any enemy encampments?[167]

When a person admits a sin, use the Bible to apply the gospel. For example, if it's a secret sin, you might point the person to: "He has delivered us from the domain of darkness and transferred us to the kingdom of his beloved Son, in whom we have redemption, the forgiveness of sins" (Colossians 1:13–14). Next, ask if they are willing to confess their sin to God, turn from it in repentance, submit to God, and seek his enabling power to not fall back into it again.

Whenever a captive is freed from sin, give glory together to the triune God!

Faith in Christ. All unbelievers are demonized to some degree. "In their case *the god of this world* has blinded the minds of the unbelievers, to keep them from seeing the light of the gospel of the glory of Christ, who is the image of God" (2 Corinthians 4:4). So your mission is to preach the gospel. Remember that "faith comes from hearing, and hearing through the word of Christ" (Romans 10:17). An unbeliever can only come to faith by hearing the news about Jesus Christ. So tell them. Here is the essence of the gospel:

> *God, being both holy and loving, looked upon hope-lessly sinful, rebellious mankind, and sent his Son, God in the flesh, Jesus Christ, to bear their sin, guilt, shame, condemnation, curse, wrath, and punishment on the cross. Christ's victory over sin was confirmed by his bodily resurrection so that everyone who believes in him can be assured of being reconciled to God forever. Those who are united to Christ by authentic faith will be transformed into his likeness as they grow in him.*

Demonized *believers* also need to be reminded of the gospel. When a Christian is in a battle with sin and Satan, it is all too easy to forget the gospel. So direct their faith to Christ, and Christ alone.

Whenever faith in Christ is embraced, give glory together to the triune God!

How to Handle the Hard Cases

What if you encounter a person who manifests signs of profound demonization such as speaking with a non-human voice, entering into a trance, convulsing uncontrollably, or shrieking like a crazed animal? And what if the demon engages *you* through the mouth of the demonized person? This can and does happen, so you should be prepared to command a demon to leave.[168] But how?

You will certainly use the name of Jesus. Beyond that, many books on spiritual warfare tell you to read or recite specific sentences or phrases. But confronting a demon is not a matter of having the right incantations or formulas. It is not about winning a shouting match. In fact, two people can engage in the same type of confrontation using exactly the same words with completely different outcomes. In the end, the only right way to command a demon is to approach it with a heartfelt and exclusive reliance on Christ's authority and the Holy Spirit's power.[169]

If you make the confrontation about you and your performance, and not Christ and his performance, things can go terribly wrong in a hurry. You could end up like the seven sons of Sceva when "the man in whom was the evil spirit leaped on them, mastered all of them and over-powered them, so that they fled out of that house naked and wounded" (Acts 19:16).

Here are a few more do's and don'ts. First, what you shouldn't do:

- Do not fear the demon or the demonized person.
- Do not engage the demon in a conversation or verbally spar with it.
- Do not ask the demon its name or any questions.

But make sure you:

- Remain aware that anything a demon says is probably a lie.
- Audibly, briefly, calmly, but firmly, tell it to leave in Jesus' name.

The Bible does promise that whenever we resist the devil, he will flee from us. But we do not have the exact same kind of promise when it comes to casting out demons from others. That is, we can think about casting out demons much the same way we think about prayer. After all, the process of casting out a demon, rightly understood, involves the same degree of reliance upon God found in biblical prayer. Sometimes prayer is answered in ways that are immediate and obvious. At other times, persistence in prayer is necessary, and sometimes God's ultimate answer is to deny our request. Similarly, in Scripture a demon's departure is sometimes obvious and immediate, yet we also know that Paul's "messenger of Satan" apparently never left him. Therefore, just as with prayer, our job is to act in faith, in hope, and in line with biblical teaching, and leave the results to God.

So when you have told the demon to leave, should the demonized person show any evidence of deliverance, take the following steps:

- Call the person to openly confess all known sins, and to repent.
- Call him or her to faith in the gospel of Jesus Christ.
- Help the person permanently and completely cut any and all ties to enemy encampments by which they may have been trapped.
- Help him or her to fill the void[170] with:

1. Bible reading, study, memorization, and application
2. Prayer
3. A community of believers
4. Ongoing accountability

- Teach the person about, or direct the person toward, the vital doctrines of the Bible including:

    1. The triune nature of God
    2. The incarnation of the Son of God
    3. The meaning and application of the death and resurrection of Christ
    4. The righteousness of Christ and its role in our justification
    5. The meaning of our union with Christ by genuine faith
    6. The process of sanctification and the importance of obedience
    7. The Five Solas

By now, one thing should be clear. Biblically directed efforts to free others from demonization are perfectly in line with the Great Commission—to evangelize and make disciples.

The Special Forces

As mentioned earlier, the Bible refers to individuals who are endowed with a specific spiritual gift called "the ability to distinguish between spirits" (1 Corinthians 12:4, 10). Is anyone in your church known for having an exceptional talent for helping the demonized? Make it a priority to get to know them; someday you might need to go shoulder-to-shoulder with them.

The Bible also indicates that our "powers of discernment [are] *trained* by constant practice to distinguish good from evil" (Hebrews 5:14). Anyone can develop these "powers." One purpose of this book is to provide a platform for basic Bible training on the subject of spiritual warfare. So consider studying this book in a community setting, discussing specific applications of the Scriptures as needs arise.

Regardless of the type or level of spiritual gifting you may possess, if you are in Christ you can play a vital part in helping the demonized. So be careful, yet courageous, and never take your eyes off the victorious Christ. Jesus defeated the enemy when Satan and the rebel angels sinned. Jesus defeated the enemy when he bore your sin. And, as you will see next, Jesus will utterly defeat the enemy by finally banishing the entire kingdom of darkness from our presence forever and ever.

Nine
A STORY OF CHRIST'S GLORY

On that profoundly fateful day in the Garden of Eden, the LORD God pronounced a curse on the "ancient serpent, who is called the devil and Satan" (Revelation 12:9). It ended with these highly significant words: "I will put enmity between you and the woman, and between your offspring and her offspring; he shall bruise your head, and you shall bruise his heel (Genesis 3:15).

Here, God was foreshadowing the birth of a specific individual—a *he*. From our vantage point today it's not difficult to recognize that the One who would bruise the head of Satan is none other than Jesus Christ. This prophecy is known as "The Protoevangelium," the first announcement of the gospel. It was the promise of Satan's defeat and the beginning of good news for us.

At the cross, Satan was dealt that promised decisive blow to the head, yet today he still prowls the earth, wounded and in chains, desperately seeking to devour us while he still can. The final blow is yet to come and the devil "knows that his time is short" (Revelation 12:12). In fact, the entire kingdom of darkness is painfully aware that their days of tempting, deceiving, and demonizing the human race are numbered. When Jesus encountered a legion of demons, they asked, "What have you to do with us, O Son of God? Have you come here to torment us *before the time*?" (Matthew 8:29).

What future torment are they dreading? Jesus described it as "unquenchable, eternal fire, prepared for the devil and his angels" (Mark 9:43; Matthew 25:41), a place where there will be "weeping and gnashing of teeth" (Matthew 13:42), "where their worm does not die" (Mark 9:48).

Hell is not a place of annihilation where at some point the demons will simply cease to exist. Instead, "[they will be] thrown into the lake of fire… where… they will be tormented day and night forever and ever" (Revelation 20:10). What began with a bruising of Satan's head will culminate in a constant, continuous, and conscious exacting of divine justice for the willful rebellion of fallen angels against their Creator and rightful owner, the triune God.

Will they go into the lake of fire without a struggle? No. "They will make war on the Lamb, and the Lamb will conquer them, for he is Lord of lords and King of kings, and those with him are called and chosen and faithful" (Revelation 17:14). Indeed, this war began in the Garden of Eden itself, and our Savior, Jesus, is both the Lamb and the victorious conqueror, the effectual cause of the enemy's doom.

Here's how spiritual warfare will ultimately conclude: "Then comes the end, when [Jesus] delivers the kingdom to God the Father after destroying every rule and every authority and power. For he must reign until he has put

all his enemies under his feet" (1 Corinthians 15:24–25).
When will all this happen? The Bible does not provide
a date. What will it look like? The Bible offers many
glimpses, including this rapid-fire series of astounding
metaphors:

> Then I saw heaven opened, and behold, a white
> horse! The one sitting on it is called Faithful and True,
> and in righteousness he judges and makes war.
>
> His eyes are like a flame of fire, and on his head
> are many diadems, and he has a name written that
> no one knows but himself. He is clothed in a robe
> dipped in blood, and the name by which he is called is
> The Word of God.
>
> And the armies of heaven, arrayed in fine linen,
> white and pure, were following him on white horses.
> From his mouth comes a sharp sword with which to
> strike down the nations, and he will rule them with a
> rod of iron. He will tread the winepress of the fury of
> the wrath of God the Almighty.
>
> On his robe and on his thigh he has a name
> written, King of kings and Lord of lords. (Revelation
> 19:11–16)

By now you are probably wondering—and maybe
not for the first time—why did God allow the kingdom
of darkness to develop and deceive and devour in the first
place? Why not cast Satan and his demons into the lake of
fire the moment after they rebelled?

God works all things according to the counsel of his
will.[171] And remember, it is the Father's will to glorify the
Son.[172] Defeating the enemy with immediate, raw power

at the moment the serpent succeeded in tempting Adam and Eve would in some sense have revealed the glory of the Son. But compare this to an extended timeline revealing his humility, servanthood, suffering, and death, followed by his resurrection, ascension, session, and triumphant second coming to utterly and permanently defeat the enemy. This approach would display far greater magnitudes and far more facets of the glory of Christ. For in addition to revealing his power, this extended timeline glorifies his love, patience, grace, sovereignty, and wisdom.

In other words, Christ is seen as more glorious because Satan and demons have been allowed to exist. This is also to your benefit. The more honored the Son is, the more joy is experienced by those who love him.

So in the final analysis, we see that from the Garden to the moment the enemy is cast into the lake of fire, spiritual warfare is not primarily a story about believers dressed in awesome armor. Nor is it primarily a story about Satan and demons. Instead, spiritual warfare is first and foremost a story about Christ and his all-surpassing glory over and above the kingdom of darkness. Humans and angels, both holy and fallen, are merely supporting actors in this much greater drama.

And the best part is that this drama is no cliffhanger. Through Scripture you have been shown its past, present, *and* future. Knowing the outcome of the story—Christ victorious—gives you hope when you are in the trenches and tempted to worry that Satan may win. The next time you are harassed or hindered by the enemy, remember: "The God of peace will soon crush Satan *under your feet*" (Romans 16:20).

And never forget: "You are a chosen race, a royal

priesthood, a holy nation, a people for his own possession, that you may proclaim the excellencies of him who called you out of darkness into his marvelous light" (1 Peter 2:9). Therefore,

> Be sober-minded; be watchful. Your adversary the devil prowls around like a roaring lion, seeking someone to devour. Resist him, firm in your faith, knowing that the same kinds of suffering are being experienced by your brotherhood throughout the world. And after you have suffered a little while, the God of all grace, who has called you to his eternal glory in Christ, will himself restore, confirm, strengthen, and establish you. To him be the dominion forever and ever. Amen. (1 Peter 5:8–11)

To the victorious Christ whose dominion is invincible and everlasting over all things—including Satan and demons and you and me—to him be glory forever. So may your voice forever join the holy angels, "numbering myriads of myriads and thousands of thousands, saying with a loud voice,

> *Worthy is the Lamb who was slain, to receive power and wealth and wisdom and might and honor and glory and blessing!* (Revelation 5:11–12)

Appendix 1: Learning from Your Enemy's Names

God intends for you to know about your enemy. That is why the Bible provides dozens of descriptive names for Satan and his cohorts. Each name listed below provides unique and valuable insight into the enemy's character and nature:

Abaddon/Apollyon: Satan is the king of destruction and the bottomless pit. See Job 26:6, 28:22, 31:12; Psalm 88:11; Proverbs 15:11, 27:20; Revelation 9:11.

Accuser: Like a prosecuting attorney, Satan charges redeemed humans with sin and attempts to condemn and discredit them before God's throne. See Job 1:9–11, 2:5; Zechariah 3:1; Revelation 12:10.

Antichrist: Against, opposite of, or in place of Christ. See 1 John 2:18, 22, 4:3; 2 John 1:7.

Beelzebul: Satan is the lord of the dunghill. See Matthew 10:25, 12:24, 27; Mark 3:22; Luke 11:15–19.

Belial: Useless, worthless. See 2 Corinthians 6:15.

Deceiver: By Satan's very nature he defrauds, deludes, cheats, and misleads. See Revelation 12:9, 20:3, 8.

Demon: Any fallen angel; an unclean or evil spirit—three occurrences in the OT; seventy-five in the NT.

Devil: Slanderer. Satan stirs up false witness and seeks to ruin the reputations of God and man—thirty-four references in the NT.

Dragon: Creature symbolic of Satan's ferocious evil forces intent on devouring the Messiah and his people. See Ezekiel 29:3; Isaiah 27:1; Revelation 12:1–17, 13:2–4, 11, 16:13, 20:2.

Evil one: Satan is the ultimate personal concentration and manifestation of evil and corruption. See Matthew 13:19, 38–39; John 17:15; Ephesians 6:16; 2Thessalonians 3:3; 1 John 2:13–14, 3:12, 5:18–19.

Father of lies: Satan is the patriarch and originator of false witness. See John 8:44.

God of this world: Satan is the false deity propped up and worshipped by all humanity that is set in opposition to God. See 2 Corinthians 4:4.

Murderer: From the beginning of human history, Satan's goal was to kill Jesus—and us. See John 8:44.

Prince of demons: Satan is the royal leader over the fallen angels that inhabit the dark kingdom. See Matthew 9:34, 12:24; Mark 3:22; Luke 11:15.

Prince of the power of the air: Seems to suggest that Satan's throne is in the lowest realm of the heavens, the atmospheric realm of the air above the earth. See Ephesians 2:2.

Ruler of this world: Satan is the false authority propped up and obeyed by all humanity that is set in opposition to God. See John 12:31, 14:30, 16:11.

Satan: Adversary, accuser. He opposes God's agenda and assaults God's people—fourteen references in the in OT; thirty-five in the NT.

Serpent: Satan is a cunning creature who quietly sneaks up on its prey, often with fatal results. See Genesis 3:1–14; 2 Corinthians 11:3; Revelation 12:9, 20:2.

Tempter: Satan exploits the God-given desires of humans and entices them to find fulfillment in ungodly, artificial, selfish ways. See Matthew 4:1–3; 1 Thessalonians 3:5.

Thief: Satan steals that which rightfully belongs to Christ and his people. See John 10:10.

Appendix 2: Verses for Memorization

Memorizing Scripture is not as difficult as it may seem. A good way to start is to break the passage into bite-sized pieces. Think about each word one-by-one. Turn this process into a conversation with God by praying over the words and asking him to enlighten you to the meaning. Then consider how the words and phrases can be applied to your life.

Once you have worked through this process, here are some practical tips to help you commit a passage to memory:

- Say the words aloud, over and over.
- Write out the words, over and over.
- Pair up with a like-minded believer to recite the words to one another.
- Repeat any of these steps until you have the passage memorized.

- Set up a system to periodically review each of your memory verses.

Here are some key passages that were covered in this book:

Jeremiah 2:11–13	Matthew 6:13
Matthew 28:18	John 8:12, 34–36, 44
John 12:31–33	John 16:33
Romans 1:16–17	Romans 8:1–2
Romans 8:37–39	Romans 16:20
1 Corinthians 15:3–6	1 Corinthians 15:54–58
2 Corinthians 4:4–7	2 Corinthians 10:3–5
2 Corinthians 11:14–15	2 Corinthians 12:9–10
Galatians 2:20–21	Galatians 5:16–17
Galatians 6:14	Ephesians 2:1–10
Ephesians 6:10–13	Philippians 3:7–9
Colossians 1:13–20	Colossians 2:8–10, 13–15
Colossians 3:1–4	2Timothy 2:25–26
Hebrews 2:14–15, 18	Heb. 4:14–16
James 1:12–18	James 2:19
James 4:6-8	1 Peter 5:6–11
1 John 3:8	1 John 4:1–4
1 John 5:4–5	1 John 5:18–19
Revelation 12:10–11	

Endnotes

1. 2 Timothy 3:16; 1 Corinthians 4:6
2. 2 Corinthians 2:11
3. 2 Corinthians 11:14
4. Psalm 103:19; John 18:36; Revelation 17:14, 19:16
5. Including related expressions such as *kingdom of heaven*.
6. Colossians 1:13
7. Ephesians 6:13; 1 Peter 5:8–9
8. Jesus uses the personal pronoun, *he*, to describe Satan in Matthew 12:26, Mark 3:26, and Luke 22:31. Paul uses similar personal pronouns in 2 Corinthians 2:11, 11:14.
9. Mind- Matthew 16:23; will- Matthew 4:9; emotions- Revelation 12:12; heart- Isaiah 14:13
10. A parallel meaning of this passage refers to the king of Babylon. But since Jesus connected it with Satan, we can be assured it applies to him as well.
11. See Appendix 1 for a more complete list of the names of Satan.
12. John 14:30; 2 Corinthians 4:4; 1 John 5:19b
13. A parallel meaning of this passage refers to the king of Tyre. But because of the reference to his presence in the Garden of Eden, and his identity as an extraordinary angel (cherub) who became filled with violence, sinned, and was cast away from the holy mountain of God, we can be assured it applies to Satan as well.
14. Nowhere does the Bible teach that demons are wicked humans who have died and returned to earth, or a race of humans that lived prior to Adam and Eve. See Appendix 1 for a more complete list of biblical names of Satan and demons.
15. Luke 22:3, Matthew 8:31–32
16. Hebrews 12:22, Revelation 5:11. *Myriad* can mean countless or an extremely large number.
17. Revelation 12:4. In the Bible, stars sometimes symbolize angels. For example, see Revelation 1:20, Isaiah 14:13. In our own galaxy, the number of stars is generally estimated to be at least 100 billion, and this is not to mention the billions of other galaxies. This is just one more indication that the number of angels, and thus of fallen angels, may be unimaginably large.
18. See also Psalm 106:35–37. This continued in the early church (1 Corinthians 10:20) and still exists today.
19. Matthew 12:25–26, Ephesians 6:12
20. Genesis 1:27

21. The serpent is Satan. The connection is established in Revelation 12:9.
22. Genesis 3:7–24   **23.** Psalm 51:5   **24.** Ephesians 2:2–3
25. John 17:20   **26.** John 18:36   **27.** John 15:18–19
28. *Pluralism* is the belief that all religions and belief systems are equally valid.
29. *Relativism* is the belief that there is no such thing as absolute truth.
30. 1 Corinthians 2:2   **31.** Colossians 3:1–2   **32.** Philippians 4:8
33. 2 Timothy 2:3–4   **34.** 1 John 4:4   **35.** 1 Peter 2:11
36. At times, the Bible does use "the flesh" to refer to the human body (see 2 Corinthians 10:3). But primarily the phrase is used in the spiritual sense described here, or in related ways (e.g., Romans 8:8).
37. Romans 6:23   **38.** Galatians 5:19–21
39. Matthew 5:21–22, 27–28   **40.** Colossians 2:20–23
41. John 14:26, 15:26; Romans 8:9, 11; 1 Corinthians 3:16, 6:19
42. Romans 7:24–25a
43. Hebrews 4:15, 7:26; 1 Peter 2:22; 1 John 3:5
44. 1 Peter 2:24, Colossians 2:13–14
45. 2 Corinthians 3:18   **46.** Galatians 2:21
47. Ephesians 6:16   **48.** Acts 5:3
49. Matthew 1:20. Angels can appear in dreams. It probably follows that demons can, too.
50. 2 Corinthians 10:5   **51.** 1 Samuel 13:14
52. The consequence of David's satanically inspired sin was that 70,000 people died!
53. Jeremiah 17:9
54. Psalm 145:16; Romans 11:36; 1 Corinthians 8:6
55. Hebrews 11:1, 6   **56.** Matthew 6:13
57. James 1:2–4, 12–13   **58.** 1 Peter 1:6–9
59. Hebrews 12:3–4
60. Matthew 4:1–11; Hebrews 7:26; 1 Peter 2:22; 1 John 3:5; John 8:29, 46
61. Revelation 12:10; Zechariah 3:1
62. In Job 1:9, 2:5, it is clear Job was unaware this argument was taking place.
63. Galatians 3:10b, James 2:10
64. 1 John 2:1; 1 Timothy 2:5; Hebrews 7:25
65. 1 Peter 2:24, Romans 4:5, 8:1
66. Colossians 2:13–14, Hebrews 8:12, Jeremiah 31:34, John 19:30
67. Ephesians 2:8–9

68. John 16:8–10   **69.** Romans 2:14–16, Hebrews 9:14
70. 1 Corinthians 1:9; 2 Corinthians 5:19
71. John 14:16, 26 (New American Standard Version)
72. Romans 8:15–16   **73.** Romans 5:8   **74.** John 10:28–30
75. Exodus 3:14, Isaiah 46:9a   **76.** Matthew 4:10
77. Luke 8:26–40, cf Matthew 8:32. A legion ranged from 3,000–6,000 in number.
78. Ephesians 6:10–11   **79.** Luke 10:17, 20
80. Psalm 139:4   **81.** 1 Peter 1:12
82. Job 1:7–11. In this example Satan had personally observed Job during his going "to and fro" and "up and down" upon the earth. Satan knows all about Job without the LORD telling him.
83. Also see Psalm 139:7–10
84. The words *demon* or *demons* appear 68 times in the New Testament, each time indicating a presence on earth.
85. James 4:7. Note: this verse is further biblical proof that Satan and demons are not omnipresent.
86. Luke 4:13   **87.** Ephesians 1:11   **88.** Job 1:1–2:10
89. John 14:30   **90.** Mark 1:27b
91. John 3:35, 17:2   **92.** Genesis 4:1–16
93. Matthew 16:27, Hebrews 9:27
94. 1 John 3:8   **95.** Ephesians 4:26–27
96. 1 Corinthians 7:5   **97.** James 3:14–15   **98.** 1 Timothy 6:9–10
99. Psalm 106:36
100. Although, to learn more about these dangerous temptations, see *Hit List: Taking Aim at the Seven Deadly Sins*, by Brian Hedges (Cruciform Press, 2014).
101. Exodus 20:3–4   **102.** Jeremiah 2:11–13
103. If this describes you, please read chapter 8 carefully and make sure you have a lot of prayer support.
104. 1 John 4:1–3   **105.** 2 Peter 2:1
106. Colossians 2:8   **107.** Galatians 1:6–9
108. Revelation 22:18–19; 1 Corinthians 4:6; 2 Timothy 3:16–17
109. For example, a high school graduation is a ceremony, but it is not spiritual/occult in nature, while a Christian marriage involves a ceremony, covenant, vow, promise, oath, and pledge that are explicitly spiritual, yet approved of in Scripture. When it comes to, for example, an Islamic wedding, we reiterate our perspective on occult practices: it can be biblically legitimate and spiritually safe for Christians to attend, for purposes of relationship and evangelism, without actively participating in the ceremony or explicitly approving of the underlying beliefs.

110. In the English Standard Version, examples of *daimonizomai* being translated "possessed" include Matthew 8:28, Mark 5:15, and Luke 8:36, and examples of it being translated "oppressed" include Matthew 4:24, 8:16, and Mark 1:32.
111. 1 Thessalonians 2:18; 2 Corinthians 12:7
112. Romans 11:36; 1 Corinthians 8:6; Colossians 1:16
113. Mark 1:23–26
114. Job 42:10–17
115. Luke 22:31–33
116. Matthew 16:18
117. Luke 4:1–13
118. Matthew 4:10–11
119. Luke 4:14
120. Hebrews 4:15–16
121. Mark 5:9–13
122. Luke 4:34
123. Luke 4:41
124. Mark 5:7
125. James 2:19
126. In context, destroying "the works of the devil" means destroying *sin* in the devil and in us, too.
127. Matthew 12:28–29
128. See also 1 Corinthians 15:3–9
129. John 11:25
130. John 10: 28-30
131. James 4:7
132. 2 Corinthians 5:17
133. Galatians 3:26
134. Philippians 3:20
135. John 15:15
136. Ephesians 2:5–6
137. John 16:33
138. Matthew 28:18
139. Galatians 1:4
140. Colossians 2:14–15
141. 2 Timothy 3:16–17
142. Philippians 3:9, Galatians 2:21, Romans 10:4
143. Philippians 3:9
144. 1 Peter 3:15
145. The Five Solas originated in 1554 when Melanchthon wrote, "sola gratia justificamus et sola fide justificamur" (only by grace do you justify and only by faith are we justified). The

expression has gained popularity over the centuries as a concise consensus statement of what Scripture actually teaches about the means and nature of salvation.

146. 2 Timothy 3:16; 2 Peter 1:20–21; Hebrews 4:12
147. Philippians 2:8–10
148. Matthew 26:53
149. Philippians 2:8
150. Colossians 1:27
151. Ephesians 4:27
152. Matthew 6:13
153. Mark 6:7, 13
154. Luke 10:17–20
155. Mark 1:23–26
156. Matthew 7:21–23
157. The ESV Study Bible footnotes indicate: "Mark 16:9–20 should be read with caution. As in many translations, the editors of the ESV have placed the section within brackets, showing their doubts as to whether it was originally part of what Mark wrote, but also recognizing its long history of acceptance by many in the church. The content of verses 9–20 is best explained by reference to other passages in the Gospels and the rest of the NT. Most of its content is found elsewhere, and no point of doctrine is affected by the absence or presence of verses 9–20."
158. 1 Corinthians 15:25–28
159. Although it was after Christ ascended, Paul likewise received a similar command. See Acts 26:17–18.
160. Luke 10:1–12, 17–20
161. 1 Corinthians 12:4, 10
162. Psalm 119:11
163. Ephesians 6:10
164. Galatians 6:1
165. Ephesians 5:11
166. Luke 24:46–47, Acts 26:20
167. See chapter five, "Enemy Encampments," and Appendix 2
168. Of course, for this we will need to turn to the four God-inspired books that inform us on this subject, namely, Matthew, Mark, Luke, and Acts.
169. Matthew 12:28, Luke 11:20
170. Luke 11:24–26
171. Ephesians 1:11
172. Philippians 2:9–11

The Most Encouraging Book on Hell Ever

by Thor Ramsey

The biblical view of hell is under attack. But if hell freezes over, we lose a God of love and holiness, the good new of Jesus Christ, and more. / This book was written because hell glorifies God.

97 pages
Learn more at bit.ly/HELLBOOK

"Is the fear of God merely an Old-Testament doctrine? Does hell glorify God? Will we party with Pol Pot, Vlad the Impaler, Stalin, the Marquis de Sade, and Satan in heaven? And what about Bill Maher? For answers to these and other questions, this thought-provoking, bracing corrective to the soapy bromides of recent volumes on this subject may be just the ticket. And have we mentioned that it's entertaining and encouraging?"
Eric Metaxas, New York Times Best-selling author of **Bonhoeffer: Pastor, Martyr, Prophet, Spy**

"*The Most Encouraging Book on Hell Ever* is also one of the wisest. This book is crammed with hilarious quips, but the message is deadly serious. Losing the doctrine of hell isn't trivial. It means losing truth, righteousness, and grace. Ultimately it means losing God. Thor's book uses humor to disarm readers just enough to deliver this crucial and timely message."
Drew Dyck, managing editor of **Leadership Journal**, *a* **Christianity Today** *publication*

"'Praise God for Thor! The end must be getting near as Christians are actually getting funny. After a few pages, you'll realize this ain't your grandma's book about hell... but she'd love it just the same. Because it's only funny in the right places."
Stephen Baldwin, actor, author, radio host

The Two Fears
Tremble Before God Alone

by Chris Poblete

**You can fear God...
or everything else.**

**Only one fear brings life and hope,
wisdom and joy.**

Fear wisely.

*92 pp.
Learn more at bit.ly/2FEARS*

"We are too scared. And we aren't scared enough. Reading this book
will prompt you to seek in your own life the biblical tension between
'fear not' and 'fear God.'"

Russell D. Moore, Dean, Southern Baptist Theological Seminary

"An importantly counter-cultural book, moving us beyond a
homeboy God we could fist-bump to a holy God we can worship.
The Two Fears helps us recover a biblical fear of God and all the awe,
repentance, and freedom from self-centered fears that go with it. An
awesome resource!"

Dr. Thaddeus Williams, professor, Biola University

"In this practical and very readable book, Chris Poblete shows how
both the absence of true fear and the presence of 'unholy [false] fear'
stem from an absence of a knowledge of the awesome God of the
Bible, and that, in meeting him, we discover the real dimensions of
creational existence and the wonderful benefits of living in fear and
deep respect before him, freed from the '[false] fear of men.'"

*Peter Jones, Ph.D., TruthXchange; Scholar-in-Residence and
Adjunct Professor, Westminster Seminary in California*

"I commend this book to you: it will fuel your worship and empower
your discipleship."

Gabe Tribbett, Christ's Covenant Church, Winona Lake, IA

Licensed to Kill
A Field Manual for Mortifying Sin

by Brian G. Hedges

Your soul is a war zone.
Know your enemy.
Learn to fight.

101 pp. Learn more at bit.ly/L2Kill

"A faithful, smart, Word-centered guide."
  – *Wes Ward, Revive Our Hearts*

"Are there things you hate that you end up doing anyway? Have you tried to stop sinning in certain areas of your life, only to face defeat over and over again? If you're ready to get serious about sin patterns in your life—ready to put sin to death instead of trying to manage it—this book outlines the only strategy that works. This is a book I will return to and regularly recommend to others."
  ***Bob Lepine, Co-Host*, FamilyLife Today**

"Brian Hedges shows the importance of fighting the sin that so easily entangles us and robs us of our freedom, by fleeing to the finished work of Christ every day. Well done!"
  ***Tullian Tchividjian, Coral Ridge Presbyterian Church; author,* Jesus + Nothing = Everything**

"Rather than aiming at simple moral reformation, *Licensed to Kill* aims at our spiritual transformation. Like any good field manual, this one focuses on the most critical information regarding our enemy, and gives practical instruction concerning the stalking and killing of sin. This is a theologically solid and helpfully illustrated book that holds out the gospel confidence of sin's ultimate demise."
  ***Joe Thorn, pastor and author,* Note to Self: The Discipline of Preaching to Yourself**

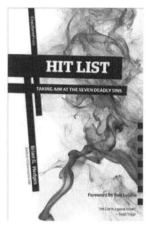

Hit List
Taking Aim at the Seven Deadly Sins

by Brian G. Hedges

Pride, envy, wrath, sloth, greed, gluttony, lust: Not just corrupting vices, but gateway sins leading to countless others. Learn how to take aim at each one. Reach for holiness.

112 pp.
Learn more at bit.ly/HITLIST-7

"*Hit List* is a great book! Hedges brings the historic framework of the seven deadly sins into the 21st century. Brian's reading and research into historic Christian theology enriches this readable and thoroughly biblical examination and treatment of 'the big seven.'"
Tedd Tripp, author, conference speaker

"Satan destroys by cloaking his schemes in darkness. *Hit List* is a blazing floodlight—both convicting and gleaming with gospel clarity. For the Christian soldier eager to win the daily war against sin, *Hit List* is a welcome field manual."
Alex Crain, Editor, Christianity.com

"If you've ever heard you shouldn't envy (or get angry or lust or ...), but you don't know exactly what those sins look like in your everyday life—let alone the cure—then *Hit List* is for you. Brian has done his research, and I'm personally grateful for his insights on what's at the root of specific sins I deal with...and how I can break free. Read, repent, and live free!"
Paula Hendricks, Editorial Manager, Revive Our Hearts

"With characteristic depth, Brian unpacks an ancient formulation of our soul-sickness, while giving us the antidote of grace and gospel."
Del Fehsenfeld III, Senior Editor, Revive magazine

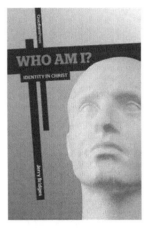

Who Am I?
Identity in Christ
by Jerry Bridges

Jerry Bridges unpacks Scripture to give the Christian eight clear, simple, interlocking answers to one of the most essential questions of life.

91 pp.
Learn more at bit.ly/WHOAMI

"Jerry Bridges' gift for simple but deep spiritual communication is fully displayed in this warm-hearted, biblical spelling out of the Christian's true identity in Christ."

J. I. Packer, *Theological Editor,* ESV Study Bible; *author,* Knowing God, A Quest for Godliness, Concise Theology

"I know of no one better prepared than Jerry Bridges to write *Who Am I?* He is a man who knows who he is in Christ and he helps us to see succinctly and clearly who we are to be. Thank you for another gift to the Church of your wisdom and insight in this book."

R.C. Sproul, *founder, chairman, president, Ligonier Ministries; executive editor,* Tabletalk *magazine; general editor,* The Reformation Study Bible

"*Who Am I?* answers one of the most pressing questions of our time in clear gospel categories straight from the Bible. This little book is a great resource to ground new believers and remind all of us of what God has made us through faith in Jesus. Thank the Lord for Jerry Bridges, who continues to provide the warm, clear, and biblically balanced teaching that has made him so beloved to this generation of Christians."

Richard D. Phillips, *Senior Minister, Second Presbyterian Church, Greenville, SC*

Contend
Defending the Faith in a Fallen World

by Aaron Armstrong

Every generation must contend for the faith.

We don't want to miss the mark.

Be merciful. Be uncompromising.

Contend!

91 pp.
Learn more at bit.ly/CONTEND

"Exactly the kind of book the church needs in our moment. We are tempted today on every side to be meek as a mouse. Armstrong's gospel-saturated writing, coupled with deeply instructive practical examples, will equip the church to be as bold as a lion, and to roar as Luther, Calvin, Spurgeon and Machen before us."
Owen Strachan, Assistant Professor, Boyce College

"Here is a balanced and passionate appeal, especially to young people, to take seriously their commitment to Jesus in all areas of life, both individually and in community, contending for the Faith, using both their minds and their hearts in defense of the Truth, in the manner laid out by the apostle Jude. May this call be heard far and wide."
Dr. Peter Jones, Executive Director, truthXchange

"A fine combination of concise biblical exposition, down-to-earth examples, contemporary illustrations, and challenging practical application. It's not only an ideal book for discipling a new believer, but also for shaking the more mature out of dangerous complacency and passivity."
David P. Murray, Puritan Reformed Theological Seminary

"Helps us understand why it's hard to take a stand, what's worth fighting for, and how to do it. I'm grateful for this biblical and helpful book."
Darryl Dash, Pastor and blogger at Dashhouse.com

Knowable Word
Helping Ordinary People Learn to Study the Bible

by Peter Krol
Foreword by Tedd Tripp

Observe...Interpret...Apply. Simple concepts at the heart of good Bible study. Learn the basics in a few minutes—gain skills for a lifetime. The spiritual payoff is huge. Ready?

117 pages
Learn more at bit.ly/Knowable

"*Knowable Word* is valuable for those who have never done in-depth Bible study and a good review for those who have. I look forward to using this book to improve my own Bible study....a great service."
Jerry Bridges, author and speaker

"It is hard to over-estimate the value of this tidy volume. It is clear and uncomplicated. No one will be off-put by this book. It will engage the novice and the serious student of Scripture. It works as a solid read for individuals or as an exciting study for a small group."
Tedd Tripp, pastor and author (from the Foreword)

"At the heart of *Knowable Word* is a glorious and crucial conviction: that understanding the Bible is not the preserve of a few, but the privilege and joy of all God's people. Peter Krol's book demystifies the process of reading God's Word and in so doing enfranchises the people of God. I warmly encourage you to read it. Better still, read it with others and apply its method together."
Dr. Tim Chester, The Porterbrook Network

"Here is an excellent practical guide to interpreting the Bible. Krol has thought through, tested, and illustrated in a clear, accessible way basic steps in interpreting the Bible, and made everything available in a way that will encourage ordinary people to deepen their own study."
Vern Poythress, Westminster Theological Seminary